This Side of the River

A CENTENNIAL STORY
SALEM COVENANT CHURCH
1888-1988

Glen V. Wiberg
with sketches by LaVonne Ecker

This book is dedicated to the unnamed saints in Salem's story on the other side of the river.

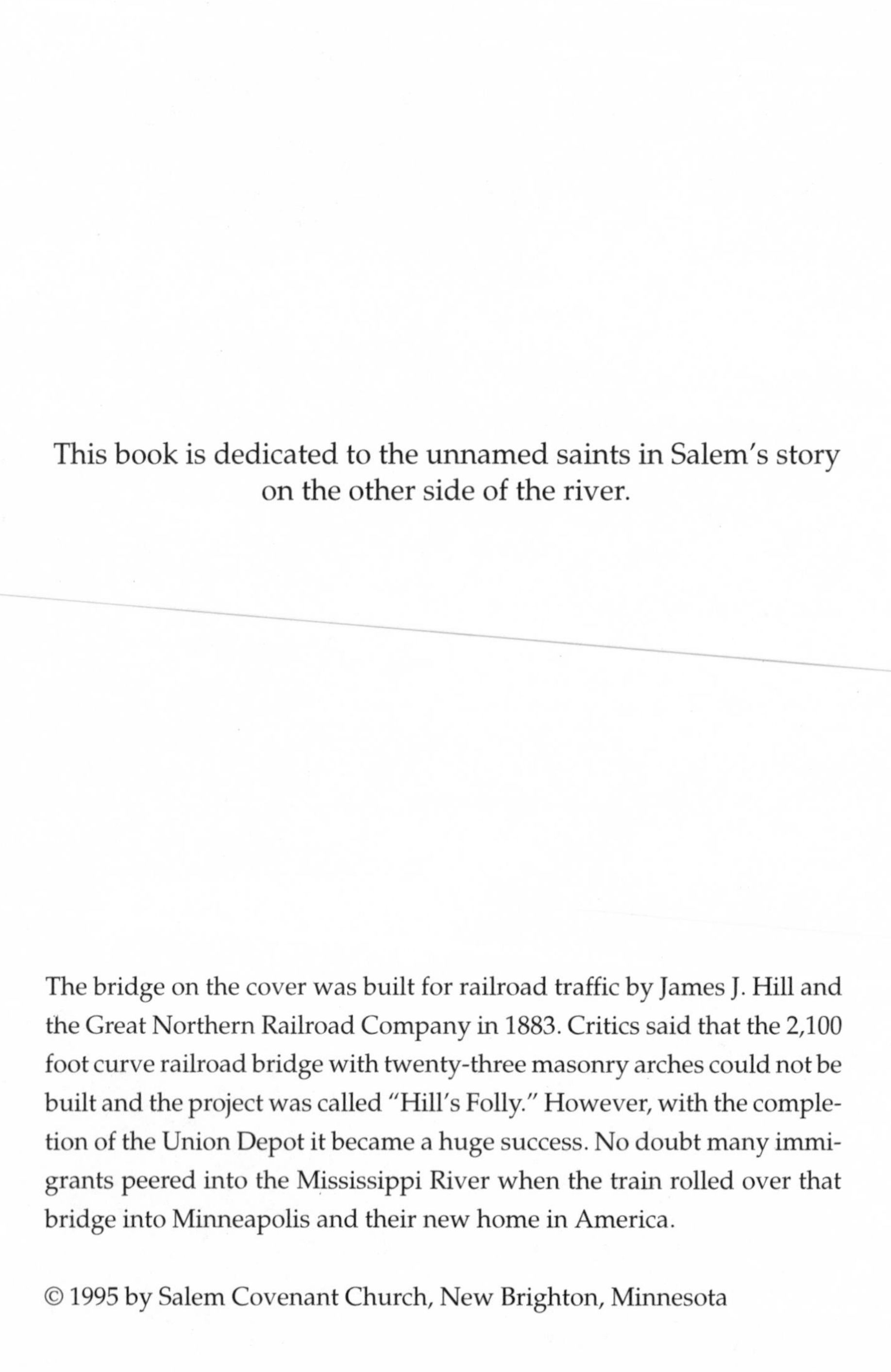

The bridge on the cover was built for railroad traffic by James J. Hill and the Great Northern Railroad Company in 1883. Critics said that the 2,100 foot curve railroad bridge with twenty-three masonry arches could not be built and the project was called "Hill's Folly." However, with the completion of the Union Depot it became a huge success. No doubt many immigrants peered into the Mississippi River when the train rolled over that bridge into Minneapolis and their new home in America.

Contents

Foreword

The account of Salem Covenant Church which follows is complete in itself and has its own interest, drama, and religious thrust. But a reminder of what the rest of Minneapolis, of Minnesota, and even of the United States was like might be fascinating and informative, too. The materials from Minnesota history are both abundant and exceedingly varied in kind.

The single best book on the entire Minnesota story, especially for the period of Salem Church's history, is Theodore C. Blegen's *Minnesota, A History of the State*. Professor Blegen's father was himself an immigrant from Norway and the founder of Augsburg College in Minneapolis. That college and its supporting Norwegian Lutherans were somewhat like the Covenant people among the Swedish: intent upon Martin Luther's understanding of the Bible and the church and zealous for a personal faith and pious living. In consequence, Professor Blegen is very sensitive to the religious life of immigrant groups in Minnesota.

A massive but readable four-volume work by William W. Folwell called simply *History of Minnesota* (published from 1921 to 1930) is the culmination of decades of work by Minnesota's most revered scholar, educator, and university president. It tells the story of Minnesota's origins: the explorations of English and French adventurers and the formation of government, social life, statehood (in 1858), and, of course, religious life and institutions. Together these books remind us how complex and rich the historical scene was for earnest people coming from abroad. Slight wonder that many felt like outsiders, that like Ole Rölvaag (in *Giants in the Earth*) they wondered if immigrants had souls. Obviously, they did. For as they tended to their physical needs and made homes and communities for themselves, they also cultivated their religious lives and aims.

It is well to remember that the area we now call Minnesota was carved out of three governmental areas: the Northwest, Louisiana, and Missouri territories. Michigan became a state in the United States of America in 1837, Wisconsin in 1848, and Minnesota in 1858. Fort Snelling was begun in 1819, and it quickly became the strategic center for the development of the area. The fort became an island of safety; but more, it attracted communities of civilized people, principally from the eastern part of the United States, whose lives, arts, industry, learning, and religion were the beginnings of the burgeoning culture of the Middle West. In the course of a few years, the two largest cities of Minnesota sprang up a short distance above and below the Mississippi River from the new fort.

The population began to grow very dramatically in the 1840s. Initially the growth came from the population moving from the eastern states. People were looking for cheaper land, for other economic opportunities, and also for adventure. By 1850 there were twenty thousand new residents in the Minnesota area, plus thousands of native Americans. By 1858, when Minnesota became a state, there were 150,000 new faces. However, by 1880 there were immigrants from abroad to be reckoned with. The total population of Minnesota then was close to 800,000, of whom about 30 percent were foreign-born. Three hundred thousand were Minnesota-born, and the remainder were second-generation Americans from elsewhere in the United States. The New England influence was obviously strong in the early years of statehood. The industries, the schools and colleges, and the churches reflected both old England and New England. So Henry Whipple, a staunch New Englander with great regard for old England, became the first Episcopal bishop of the Minnesota area in 1859.

Congregationalists, Methodists, Presbyterians, Baptists, and Quakers were well represented by the 1850s. In the 1830s there were evangelists working with the American Indians near the present town of Aitken, Minnesota, and a mission house was functioning on Lake Harriet in 1835. An Episcopal mission planted by English evangelists coming down from

Canada in the 1790s became a congregation in the 1830s; it is still St. John's Episcopal Church on the Leech Lake Chippewa Indian Reservation in northern Minnesota.

The internal migrations of the restless settlers in the New World brought Catholics by the score up the Mississippi River. Mostly they were French in origin, but they too were builders and evangelists. They established the first cathedral in St. Paul in 1841. Seventy years later, after the tides of German and Irish immigrants from Europe, the third and present cathedral was built, and it still graces the Twin Cities landscape. So churches came as the people did, in all varieties and styles.

Scandinavian immigration began haltingly in the late 1840s and early 1850s, but by 1880 there were thousands of Norwegians, Swedes, and Danes pouring into the Middle West. Of course, most of them were Lutherans. However, there were different kinds of Lutherans. Some stressed the sacraments of baptism, confirmation, and Holy Communion; some were anxious to give more authority to the congregation and less to the priests (they were "free church" oriented); some put more emphasis on personal piety and less on loyalty to creeds and church traditions. And all the Lutherans of Europe, including the Germans, had had difficulties with missionary work. Their churches were allied with governments, so mission societies of a private sort, not officially related to the national churches, had grown up everywhere in northern Europe. These societies, too, came with the immigrants.

The rich stream of American church life, brought earlier by internal migrants who had come from east to west, now came to blend and sometimes to conflict with the nineteenth century immigrants' modes of life and worship. The story of the Swedish Lutheran pastor Eric Norelius, who seemed to know both sides, is a case in point. The Norwegians, on the face of it, were more successful in forming a single Lutheran church for themselves in this new country than were the Germans and the Swedes. They somehow caused their churches in America to combine missions, piety, liturgy, priests, and congregational forms of governance in ways that the others did not.

In any case, when the Swedes came to Chicago, St. Paul, Minneapolis, and elsewhere, it became a big question whether and how they should organize and conduct themselves. The Congregationalists developed a Swedish branch that brought many Scandinavians into their orbit. No wonder that some early Lutherans (in Delaware and Pennsylvania) allied themselves with Episcopalians, and early Covenant groups in the east described themselves as Swedish Congregationalists.

The groups in Minneapolis and St. Paul were different. Broad American church politics were not their concern. Eventually the Evangelical Free Church, mostly Scandinavian and like the Mission Covenant in origin, defined itself against both the Lutheran heritage and much of American Christendom. But the people who made up Salem Church seemed to want to worship God in ways they thought were both right and familiar, biblical and Swedish. That is why the ensuing story is both historically illuminating and religiously edifying.

But there is more to be said, too. The Mission Covenant churches placed great emphasis upon preaching. The content of that preaching was usually biblical themes, so construed that the gospel, the good news about God in Christ Jesus, stood forth very vividly. Amid the streams of religion in the new land, Salem Church succeeded in putting that word very near us in a wonderful way, as a song in our hearts and a confession of the lordship of Jesus on our lips. And a personal note might also be appropriate: after decades of study and inquiry in the wider scene, it is a matter of simple justice to admit that the fundamentals of Christian living were laid down by the fellowship whose history is here celebrated.

PAUL L. HOLMER

Preface

The title of the book, *This Side of the River*, refers initially to Northeast Minneapolis, separated from the central city of Minneapolis by the Mississippi River. Early histories of Salem refer to the first mission house on Jefferson Street as "the church this side of the river." Used in this sense, the phrase suggests a historic relationship to the "mother church," the Swedish Tabernacle (now First Covenant) on the other side of the river.

The three locations of Salem Covenant Church—Jefferson Street, Central Avenue, and Silver Lake Road—have not altered the accuracy of that descriptive term "this side of the river." It further suggests, by implication, the necessity of crossing the river. From earliest times the Hennepin Avenue bridge has been, in its several forms, the connecting link between the two parts of the city, Minneapolis and Northeast. The bridge itself then becomes a metaphor for making connections in a network of travel and communication.

This Side of the River also indicates that the church does not exist in isolation, either from other churches or from the city. Even in the suburb of New Brighton, the organic connection of the church with the city, in both its promise and its destiny, has not changed. The bridging of the community is even more urgent today than in the 1880s when the congregation was being formed.

The story of the church "this side of the river" is told in these pages somewhat differently than in previous anniversary histories. Rather than telling the story of Salem chronologically from 1888 to 1988, or by the history of its three buildings and locations, or even by the record of the pastors who have served the congregation through its one hundred years, the story—like traffic on a bridge—moves back and forth by reference to themes that have served to give Salem its identity. These themes have to do with the immigrant experience, building and place, preaching, worship and music, caretaking, the role of women, the strain of martyrdom, witness, evangelism, and education. Because Salem represents what a professor at North Park Seminary referred to as "a classic model of Lutheran pietism,"[1] it is our hope that the story will be of interest to a wider audience beyond the former and present members of the congregation.

What adds further interest to the Salem story are the associations the congregation had with early Covenant leaders, such as E. August Skogsbergh, C.A. Bjork, David Nyvall, Axel Mellander, P.P. Waldenstrom, A.E. Palmquist, A.L. Skoog, and others. It is noteworthy that two of Salem's pastors became presidents of the denomination, Carl Victor Bowman and Clarence A. Nelson. The latter also served as president of Minnehaha Academy and North Park College and Theological Seminary. Following his pastorate at Salem, Pastor Bowman served as superintendent of the Northwest Conference.

Other pastors have also served both conference and denomination, making significant contributions to the larger Covenant community. Two of Salem's members have been involved in the theological education of several generations of students: Professor Donald C. Frisk of North Park Theological Seminary and Dr. Paul L. Holmer of the University of Minnesota and Yale Divinity School. And one cannot be unmindful of the many members called into pastoral and missionary service from Salem, including one of four martyrs in Covenant history, missionary Martha Anderson.

While the influence of Salem in the wider religious community has been noteworthy, perhaps the most significant influence of Salem has been upon those countless numbers of lay persons who have remained faithful "in season and out of season." In speaking to high school students in the School of Christian Living in the fall of 1991, one older member spoke for many in giving witness to the impact of the church on his life:

> I sometimes think I was born at Salem. I know I was baptized there, attended Sunday school, came to acknowledge Christ as my Lord and Savior, was confirmed, attended Junior League, belonged to the Young People's Society, joined the church, served on its boards, and served as chairman of the church for a while. Now after seventy-eight years in Salem, over sixty-five of them as a member, I feel I have the right to pause, reflect, and ask, "Has all this been worthwhile?" My answer is, "Absolutely. I don't regret a moment of it." That goes both for following Jesus and for being active in the church.[2]

Telling the story of the church "this side of the river" would not have been possible for this author alone. Here tribute must be paid to those who told Salem's story in the six preceeding anniversary books:

Ett Tjugufemårsminne (Twenty-five Years Remembered), edited by Rev. C.F. Sandstrom in 1913

Minnesskrift (Written Remembrance), edited by Rev. C.A. Gavert for the fortieth anniversary in 1928

After Fifty Years, with the historical section written by Rev. Erick Dahlhielm

Builders with God, which was largely a pictorial view of Salem's past and present for the sixtieth anniversary in 1948

Footsteps in Faith, with the historical section written by Ruth Andersson for the seventy-fifth anniversary

Go Forward, written and compiled by Ruth Anderson for the ninetieth anniversary

Likewise, the present History Committee, under the tireless labor of its chairman, Curtiss D. Johnson, provided invaluable help in gathering information and telling stories, offering helpful suggestions in the group reading of the manuscript, and providing inspiration and encouragement to the author. Special mention must be made of the work of LaVonne Ecker as artist, whose sketches throughout the book both enliven the text and express her lifelong devotion to Salem; of Vernice Monson's fine work in translating early church minutes and family letters from Swedish, enabling ease of access to the early history of Salem; and of Lorraine Johnson's gracious and ever-present hospitality in providing coffee and refreshments for our committee meetings, in addition to her many hours of secretarial work. The members of the History Committee are Carl Philip Anderson, advisor, Erma Chinander, LaVonne Ecker, Phyllis Erickson, Ward Holm, Paul L. Holmer, Curtiss D. Johnson, Vernice Monson, Laurie Peterson, Bernice Stohlberg, Evelyn Strand, and Gary Schwartz.

I have been grateful for the helpful counsel of others during the writing: Philip J. Anderson, professor, North Park Seminary; Timothy Johnson, Covenant archivist; and James R. Hawkinson, former secretary of Covenant Publications. Likewise, I must express gratitude to the present pastor of Salem, Don N. Johnson, for his encouragement and support of the project, and finally to Karen Bjorklund for her extraordinary patience and labor of love in preparing the manuscript for publication.

REV. GLEN V. WIBERG
June 1, 1995

A Letter From the Author

MY DEAR GRANDCHILDREN,

Today I begin writing the story of Salem—the church where you were baptized and where you are known and loved as children of the congregation. Before beginning this undertaking, I thought it would be good to write this letter to you about how this story is already part of your story. If you know something about where we came from, then you will be able to appreciate your church more and perhaps someday tell the story to your children.

As your grandpa, I need to tell you the stories my grandpa told me when I was a boy. His name was Charles Joseph Wiberg, and he would be your great-great-grandpa. I know you would have liked him. He was everybody's grandpa. Young and old all called him Grandpa. I think of him often—the neatly trimmed mustache, the gold-rimmed glasses, the smiling blue eyes, the sandy hair with the faint, sweet smell of Lucky Tiger Hair Tonic, the big blacksmith hands, the shuffling walk, and the Swedish accent. I can still hear his fervent prayers ringing in my ears.

We shared the same bedroom when he lived with us, and I loved to hear him tell stories. No matter how many times I heard them, I always wanted to hear them again. Charles Joseph was born in the 1860s of a poor, hard-working woman who was a butcher for a wealthy land owner near Örebro, Sweden. They lived in a small cottage on a large estate. Like everyone in those days, Charlie was baptized into the state Lutheran church. In 1968 we visited that lovely rural church and saw the font where

Grandpa was baptized. It was a very moving moment for me to see the place where his spiritual journey began.

Growing up in those days was hard, especially for poor peasants. Charlie went to school for only a few months each year and never finished grade school. In order for the family to survive, he had to work as a farmhand from early morning to late at night—at least in the summer, when the days were long. The farmers he worked for were often cruel in their treatment of him. His mother, who was a believer, warned him about the evils of snuff and strong drink, pointing out examples in the neighborhood of where such a life would lead. But it was not until he was a teenager that he became a believer.

Now this is how the movement which later became the Covenant Church began. Young Charlie found himself drawn to a group who were nicknamed "readers" because of their passion to meet in small groups and read the Bible in homes. It was not like doing Bible study as we often do it today. It was reading the Bible together for the purpose of meeting God, to discover how one who is a sinner could find peace with God. Because these house meetings were without official approval, the pastor of the parish church could make life unpleasant for these readers.

On occasion, religious meetings would be held in a schoolhouse and a traveling lay person would preach. It was at such a meeting that young Charlie came to a turning point in his life—either give himself totally to Jesus now or the opportunity might never come again. Returning home, he fell on his knees in a roadside ditch and gave his life to Christ. I can't help wondering if I would be writing this letter to you today had Charlie not chosen the Way. At any rate, despite many hardships and trials he became and remained throughout his life a happy, earnest Christian.

It would take many more pages to tell you about how he left his homeland for America when he was in his early twenties. Like the thousands of Swedes and Norwegians who caught what was then called "America fever," his main reason for leaving Sweden was the chance for a better life. Grandpa took the train from Örebro to Gothenburg, then took a steamer to Hull, England, where he boarded a train to Liverpool and from there sailed to New York. That was the common route to America.

Like all immigrants, he traveled as a third-class passenger, taking with him the food and eating utensils he would need on the nine-day trip across the ocean. These included hard bread, butter, cheese, sausage, dried beef, and pickled herring, along with sugar, rusks, coffee beans, and a small pot packed into a large wicker basket. He slept on a wooden bunk in a crowded room with little privacy. It was anything but a pleasure trip. After going through customs at Ellis Island, he took a train to Kansas City, Missouri, where a boyhood friend had come earlier. There he settled in an area called Swede Hill, found a job as a blacksmith on the Sante Fe Railroad, and joined the Swedish Mission Church on Belleview Street, where he met his wife, Augusta.

There is much more I could tell you about your great-great-grandpa. But knowing something about your own family story will help you understand how thousands of other immigrants came to America, and how important for many of them was a personal, living faith in Jesus, the crucified and risen Savior—as important as daily bread. That common experience of Jesus, along with the need for being together, led these immigrants to form congregations like the one we belong to—Salem Covenant Church. I may write you another letter or two telling more of the story. But this, at least, is a beginning.

With love,

GRANDPA WIBERG
December 1, 1992

1

A Church Seeking Its Identity

A Memorable Gathering

During the year commemorating Salem's centennial, several vignettes depicting significant events in the congregation's history were included in the Sunday morning services. The first vignette, called "Early Beginnings: This Side of the River," was presented on January 31, 1988. The scene was set in the Nils Olsson home on Monroe Street near 17th Avenue in Northeast Minneapolis on a cold winter evening in late 1881. The simple props suggested the living room of an immigrant home—a wedding portrait on the wall, a table with a kerosene lamp, a wood stove, and chairs enough to seat the few people gathered. Those present were N.G. Johnson, Mr. and Mrs. Frans Larson, A.G. Erickson, John L. Blomquist, John Jungberg, and Mrs. Nils Olsson.

Mrs. Olsson was the hostess of the meeting, since her husband was working as a logger in the north woods—something common among immigrant men during winter months. The clothes were typical of the "Sunday best" of the 1880s—men in dark suits and high shirt collars, women in long, dark skirts with high-necked blouses.[1] Typical of the form which the revival movement took in Sweden, the meeting of these few believers resembled a "conventicle"—a house meeting of the religiously earnest who were nicknamed *läsare*, or readers.

Their reason for gathering on that cold winter evening was to seek Christian fellowship through prayer, singing, reading the Bible, or perhaps a sermon by Luther or an article from the publication of the new movement, *Pietisten* (The Pietist). At this particular meeting enacted in the vignette, Pastor Emil Gustaf Törnquist[2] from the only Swedish Mission Church in Minneapolis (now First Covenant) came to speak the word and lend encouragement to the "few and poor."[3]

As the story of the congregation's modest beginnings was told a hundred years later, the contrast between the meeting on Monroe Street and the spacious modern structure on Silver Lake Road could not have been greater. No longer the "few and poor," but now the many and rich—at least by immigrant standards. No longer a barren living room, but a beautifully appointed sanctuary resembling more the parish churches they had left than the mission house they would build.

But if memories were stirred by recollections of that first generation of immigrants, some of whom were known and remembered by those present on Silver Lake Road, it was more than nostalgia that was the connecting link. It was rather a common search for identity. Who were they, and who are we? If their lives were memorable and their story worthy of being told to this generation, it was in large part because of the need to ask how the church today has been shaped by their search for identity in a much different time and place. What drives that quest for present and future generations of Covenanters has to do with seeing what the forebears saw, hearing what they heard, being gripped by what held them—in short, discovering anew the living faith of those few and poor who were the seeds in the planting and flourishing of Salem. But one must attend to the soil, both where they had started and where they had been transplanted.

Of Time and Place

Those few and poor meeting on Monroe Street had been carried to this country on the greatest tide of migration the world has ever known. The high point of Swedish immigration came in 1887, when 46,252 Swedes left home for "the Promised Land."[4] They were frontier people seeking a better life economically while also looking for a place of opportunity where they could exercise values of work, home, and—in many cases—church with a greater sense of freedom. Most of the immigrants were without property or means, from remote rural areas or expanding urban centers. For many Swedes, Minnesota was a place like home, both in its climate and in its rolling countryside marked with lakes, streams, and rivers.

As they left the Old World behind, this new time and place must have seemed like the end of the world as well as its beginning. Among the earliest immigrants to come to Minnesota was Hans Mattson, who arrived in 1851. He became a colonel in the Civil War, with his own Swedish-American regiment. Later he was elected secretary of state as well as secretary of the Board of Immigration. One cannot underestimate his role in making a place for Swedish immigrants in the settlement of Minnesota.[5]

Through the eyes of those few and poor everything must have seemed virginal, like creation under way. After all, Minnesota had been received into the Union less than thirty years before.[6] Not many of them would know or appreciate that a Catholic priest, Father Louis Hennepin, was the first white man to see St. Anthony Falls, in 1630, or that the land lying between the St. Croix and Mississippi rivers, including Northeast Minneapolis, had been ceded to the United States by the Sioux and Chippewa Indians in the treaties of 1837.

"This Side of the River"

As late as 1891, according to a long-time resident of Northeast, F.L. Palmer, the only property platted to any great extent was that lying between Johnson Street and the river. The greater portion of property east of Central Avenue did not have a single street graded, nor were there sidewalks, city water, sewers, gas, or even electricity.[7] One old-time resident of Northeast, Elizabeth Rutherford, had lived in the Lincoln Hill District since 1886. She described the area as so wild and primitive that she often became lost in the underbrush and trees while making her way to the country road which is now known as Lowry Avenue. She further recalled that the vicinity of what is now Central Avenue was nothing but a large swampy quagmire in the spring and fall, owing to the melting of snow and the early rains. The water flowed down from the hills to the level ground and produced an undesirable condition.[8]

In the early 1880s Minneapolis was little more than a frontier town of lumber mills and grain elevators, standing in the shadow of proud old St. Paul. The few buildings on Central Avenue were frame, for the most part:

Dingman's Grocery Store,[9] Blankenhorn's Meat Market, Humphrey's Confectionary, Moody's Drug Store, L.W. Northfield's Feed Store, the Soo Wood and Coal Company, and the small real estate office of H.H. Smoth, which accommodated a printing office and a barber shop.

According to the recollections of P.C. Deming, who was a realtor in the early days of the East Side, 1888 saw the beginnings of a sizable expansion: "Harrison Street was opened through to lower Central and the entire avenue given the latter name. New houses and business buildings were put up in large numbers. Water mains and plank sidewalks made their appearance."[10]

From an article published in the *North East Argus* of May 20, 1893, one gets the sense of further expansion—if not a building boom—underway in the early 1890s: "More improvements are in progress this year in northeast Minneapolis than in any other part of the city. The railroad companies, the large corporations, carpenters and builders seem to be vying with each other to see which will show the most and be of the most lasting benefit to the city."[11]

"This side of the river" became fruitful soil for the many immigrants flooding into the area. Northeast was a community of working people, a developing business and industrial area with modest homes in ethnic neighborhoods populated by Russian, Polish, Italian, German, Norwegian, and Swedish immigrants. Transplanted from foreign soil, they planted themselves here, bringing with them habits of hard work and thrift, their own songs, stories, and memories, and a profound hunger for the American dream.

Lutheran "Mission Friends"

Those who gathered for the first house meeting on Monroe Street were described in the earliest history as *den troende* (the believing), and from every evidence, many of them were members of the church across the river, *Den Svenska evangeliska Lutherska missionsförsamling* (The Swedish Evangelical Lutheran mission congregation).[12] Though touched by the revival movement in Sweden and affected by winds of change that created a restless yearning for freedom from old, oppressive structures, they were still Lutherans. Disciplined by that tradition, they had in them an inborn love of order. They were firmly rooted in the historical church, with an appreciation for the many and varied polyphonic voices of Christendom. With some exceptions, these were people characterized by sobriety and balance. As Karl Olsson says of them,

> In the public schools the children of Mission Friends were instructed daily in the Shorter Catechism of Luther. They sang Lutheran psalms and heard Lutheran prayers. Many of them were confirmed by Lutheran pastors.
>
> A group of people disciplined by generations of instruction and worship in the Lutheran church and accustomed to the orderliness of life within that communion could not, however sudden or thorough-going their personal encounter with Christ, be expected to become spiritual anarchists.[13]

But they were also people of the revival. The "stone of stumbling" leading to the separation of the Mission Friends from the largest body of Swedish Lutheran immigrants, the Augustana Synod, had to do with the concept of church membership. What these few and poor wanted above all was a fellowship of believers—people who not only believed in the Scriptures and the formal Lutheran confessions, but had a personal faith in the crucified and risen Christ. More than orthodoxy, respectable conduct, baptism, and confirmation, one needed a personal meeting with the living God.

In retrospect, what appears so remarkable about these people—small in number, of a lower economic class, and most with only limited education—is how, in their indigenous reading of the Scriptures, they discovered the shape and scope, the richness and depth, of the gospel. In paying tribute to them, Eric Hawkinson says that "it is doubtful if any generation has been more certain of the centrality of grace since the disciples walked in the physical presence of Jesus."[14]

"Mother Church"

What must not be lost to the telling of Salem's story is that, from the beginning, these Mission Friends who lived in Northeast both sought and received the blessing of the "mother church" across the river. Those meeting in the Olssons' living room back in the winter of 1881 would never have thought of saying, "Well, here we are. We are believers in Christ. We have the word of God. Now let's start a church." They would not presume upon an order already established, for they knew that the church is not born of a human decision, but exists only in the mystery of God's grace mediated through the larger body.

The reason for the Monroe Street meeting was practicality as much as edification. The trek across the river to what was later known as the Swedish Tabernacle was a long distance by foot, especially in bad weather. Even

when the one-horse "bob-tail" streetcar came to Northeast a year later, the nearly one-hour trip and the nickel ride became a hardship in terms of both time and money in going to Sunday morning and evening services.[15] The mother church was sympathetic and quick to recognize the difficulty created by distance for these Mission Friends from Northeast. The presence of Pastor Emil Gustaf Törnquist, who came to speak the word and lend encouragement and support, speaks of both harmonious relationships and good order—a characteristic of Salem from that first meeting to the present.

Enter "The Firebrand"

After the sudden death of Pastor Törnquist in the spring of 1882, a young Swede was called to become pastor of the Swedish Mission Church in 1884. He had visited Minneapolis in the late 1870s, a visit which one historian said was "crowded with holy adventures." This young preacher

was Eric August Skogsbergh. Short in stature, he was rather frail looking, with thick dark hair falling back on a massive forehead. His eyes were grayish blue, sharp, and somewhat roving; his nose was of the sort Napoleon would have admired, and his thin lips were set tightly above a firm chin. Someone said that a cartoonist would have noted that the head lent itself to caricature.

His voice was clear and pleasing when he spoke or sang. But most of all, a fire burned in this young man. A passion drove him. "Go out! Go out!" was his watchword, as he urged the believers to look for souls needing to be found and gathered. In addition to being a pastor and evangelist, Skogsbergh was an architect who designed the Swedish Tabernacle. He was what one might respectfully call a religious entrepreneur. He organized just about everything, including a Swedish newspaper and a school which later became North Park College (now in Chicago).

Efforts among Northeast Mission Friends to join together with Swedish Baptists and Methodists succeeded for a while but then failed, due largely to differences in belief and practice. Renting space from a Congregational church, The Open Door Church, provided a temporary solution but soon proved too restrictive; the odd hours for meeting were inadequate for the growing numbers of those seeking the fellowship of the group.

It was Skogsbergh who cast friendly eyes on the scattered flock in Northeast and saw the prospect of one more outpost of the kingdom. A year after his arrival, the church on the other side of the river floated a loan for the Mission Friends on this side to build a place of worship at 17th Avenue and Jefferson Street. It would soon be known as "the church next to the casket factory."[16]

The economics of the situation was a further impetus leading to organization. "We were indebted to two places," recalled one member. "We paid rent for the church [on Jefferson Street] and at the same time took part in giving to the Tabernacle. Building our own congregation and church was more and more discussed."[17]

The Child Is Born

With the blessing of the mother church to organize the Mission Friends of Northeast into a congregation and withdraw from the Swedish Mission Church of Minneapolis, it is not too surprising that Skogsbergh himself was the presiding pastor at the organizational meeting on December 17, 1888.

Several notices had gone out in advance of the meeting. Despite an unusually cold winter with temperatures dropping to minus forty-seven degrees in outlying areas, thirty people were in attendance.[18] Pastor A.G. Olson, assistant to Skogsbergh, served as secretary of the meeting. The charter read as follows:

> Inasmuch as members of the Swedish Christian Mission Congregation in Minneapolis are residents of Northeast, we have come to the conclusion that it would be beneficial and necessary to organize ourselves into God's congregation, and inasmuch as a request to the above named congregation has been in friendliness granted, the undersigned have this day organized under the name: "Swedish Evangelical Mission Church of Northeast Minneapolis."[19]

Thirteen persons, all men, signed the charter:[20]

John L. Blomqvist
Adolf Ekstam
A. Gust Ericksson
Erick Ericksson
Per Hagqvist
John Hokansson
Nils Gustaf Johnsson
John Jungberg
Karl Johan Karlsson
Ludvig Lindberg
Andrew Perman
Charles L. Pearson
John Olsson

The decision that followed was twofold: to work in harmony with the members and pastors of the mother church, and to join the newly formed Swedish Evangelical Mission Covenant of America—then just three years old, with an uncertain future. Salem was, as the twenty-fifth anniversary booklet later described it, "a genuine Covenant congregation during its entire existence—not only in theory but in reality."[21] Unity and good order have marked and blessed her history.

Other housekeeping matters were taken care of, such as the election of officers, deacons, and trustees. A.G. Erickson was elected chairman, Erick Eriksson treasurer, and Charles L. Pearson secretary. The time for Sunday morning worship was set at 10:30 a.m. When the meeting finally adjourned at 1 a.m., "the child was born"![22]

The Continuing Search

In a peculiar way, the history of Salem, as we shall see, has kept the themes of the Mission Friend tradition alive. Obviously much has changed, making the discontinuities between then and now many: changes of place from Jefferson Street to Central Avenue to Silver Lake Road, social upheavals created by two world wars, the change of language from Swedish to English, and people from diverse ethnic and cultural backgrounds entering membership. Much in the lives of these Scandinavian immigrants would seem strange to us today, and doubtless much in our world would seem even stranger to them.

Yet despite vast differences, the continuities are still present. They lie in the unfolding story of Salem, in the struggle against those opposing forces that would seduce us, in the continuing struggle for identity and mission, in the love of harmonious relationships between Christian congregations, and in doing things "decently and in order." But most of all, the continuities have to do with discovering, as if for the first time, what those early Mission Friends discovered: the presence of the crucified and risen Christ within a living fellowship of believers.

2

From Mission House to Tabernacle

The Importance of Place

Out of the uprooting and displacement of nineteenth-century immigration, *place* assumed immense importance. One immigrant meeting another might begin by saying, "I was born in such-and-such a parish, in this or that province." The importance attached to where one came from indicates how place creates people. That is, place is a point of orientation, a threshold of passage, a fixed point in one's pilgrimage by which one knows his or her position in the world. Place becomes a signpost in the quest for identity.

It is equally true that people create place.[1] This occurs through memories, the telling of stories, and relationships that create a whole network of association. "I came to America with little more than the clothes on my back" was the proverbial story of the immigrant. Thus began the familiar story of adversity overcome by hard work, thrift, faith in God, and the ambition to succeed. Though not all could tell stories of success, the significance of places was nevertheless formed by the struggles of these young newcomers, whether in neighborhood, workplace, school, or church.

Sacred Places

In rabbinic tradition, the Hebrew word for *place* is also a name for God. The very place which looks so ordinary may become, as it did for Jacob, "the house of God and the gate of heaven" (Genesis 28:17). Likewise, for the immigrant, *place* came to be recognized as sacred because of the way in which it gave structure to one's experience of self and others in relation to God.

While church is the people of God on pilgrimage, and therefore more than a building, it still has an address, whether a storefront in the inner city or St. Peter's in Rome. In Salem's story the addresses have changed from 17th Avenue and Jefferson Street to 18½ and Central avenues, to Silver Lake Road and Fifth Street Northwest. These ordinary places have been made extraordinary by memories, stories, relationships, and the ritual acts which set apart each place as unique and sacred. The meeting place becomes for generations the home of the community, "the center of the world," "the gate of heaven" shaping a people in its quest for identity.

The Mission House

In the winter of 1885, under the leadership of Rev. E. August Skogsbergh, the mother church across the river made the decision to purchase two lots at the corner of 17th Avenue and Jefferson Street Northeast as an extension of its ministry.[2] The cost amounted to five hundred dollars for the first lot, and the second lot was given free of charge by a benefactor whose name is unknown.

Shortly after the purchase of the property, plans took shape for the construction of a building thirty-six by forty-eight feet, with A.G. Erickson as contractor.[3] The permit for building was granted by the inspector of buildings in Minneapolis at a cost for construction of $1,200. Because of the high degree of enthusiasm for the project by stone and cement masons, construction workers, and others who volunteered their labor, the building was completed and ready for use by the early spring of 1886. This was more than two and a half years before the congregation was officially organized.

The first sermon in the new mission house was preached by a pioneer pastor and itinerant preacher at large for the Northwest, Pastor August Bryngelson.[4] The following Sunday the church was dedicated, with Pastor S.W. Sundberg from St. Paul preaching the dedicatory sermon.[5] An overflow crowd gave an offering of $108 for the church's debt to the mother church, which still had ownership of the work.

"Simple and Plain"

During the short span of thirteen years while the congregation was located on Jefferson Street, several repairs and changes were made. An addition of twenty-six by thirty-two feet was made in 1890 at the cost of five hundred dollars—most likely for a school room and smaller meetings. In his recollections at the twenty-fifty anniversary of Salem, Skogsbergh described the church building as "most simple and plain corresponding to the period's demands."[6] Its lines reflected not only the social and economic status of the immigrant working class but the earnest desire for a simple and uncluttered faith and honesty like that of the first disciples who walked with the Lord. It was truly a *missionshus* (mission house), following the form and character of the meeting houses that the Swedish revival movement had built in protest against the old state church, which to many seemed ostentatious in its forms and ceremonies.[7]

When the congregation was organized, the building was purchased from the mother church for the sum of one thousand dollars. In the minutes following its organization, one senses a strong, compelling desire in the congregation to pay off the debt as quickly as possible. This was done by special offerings, concerts, and a subscription list among members. Stoves, chairs, and lamps were purchased, a sidewalk was laid and fencing built, and a church sign announced meeting times. Ethel Monson and Vera Jernall recalled dirt streets and wooden sidewalks that became smelly with fungus growing underneath. In the back yard was a pump for the water supply, and the necessary out-house.[8] In 1891 the Bible quotation "Behold the Lamb of God that taketh away the sins of the world" (John 1:29) was painted on the wall over the doors of the platform, thereby pointing to the essential burden of their message.

Revisiting the Past

Through a casual remark made to Curtiss Johnson by the present owner of the property on 17th and Jefferson, now a six-unit apartment complex, it was discovered that the ceiling of the old church is still intact. The original dimensions of the building can still be seen, along with a colorful stenciled border on the existing walls and ceiling. Such a discovery questions somewhat the description "simple and plain," leaving one to wonder if there was not a hunger in the human spirit for a touch of beauty, or even a wistful memory of beautiful old churches left behind in the old country.

Here I must add my own confession to the story. Climbing up a ladder through a trapdoor in the ceiling of one of the apartments, and aided by a spotlight, Curtiss and I took turns looking at the attic. Seeing the wood beams of the roof with walls and ceiling outlining the original structure inside the later addition, I felt in those moments as if historic roles had been reversed. No longer was the "great cloud of witnesses" looking down on us from some higher balcony. Now we were looking down on them. The wooden beams holding up the roof since 1886 were soaked with gospel—the singing, praying, and preaching of those immigrant forebears, few and poor, yet rich in grace.

Looking down as though through a large hole in the ceiling, I saw those people I knew who began their spiritual journeys in this place, people who were only children then: Ethel Monson, Vera Jernall, Arthur Erickson, and others, their youthful faces bright and eager with promise. I heard the voices of the early preachers, including Skogsbergh himself, fervent with gospel proclamation. Pastor August Sjöberg played his guitar and sang through a heavy bronze beard. I heard the sighs of penitence intermingled with cries of rejoicing among the newly born. I even smelled the smoke of many candles rising to the ceiling at the five o'clock Julotta service early Christmas morning, amid the strains of *Var hälsad sköna morgonstund* ("All Hail to Thee, O Blessed Morn"), the traditional chorale opening the service. And I heard Brother Lundin, the custodian, whisper into the ear of Pastor K.A. Jonson, "Preach with boldness because I and others have knelt down by the stove and cried out to God for his blessing."[9] Such was the spirit of the place!

The Tabernacle

As early as 1896 the question of building was raised again. The options were either to move the existing structure and put a basement under it, or build a new meeting house. Because of a slow but steady growth, both in membership and in ministry to children and youth, space was becoming a problem. A month before the arrival of Pastor C.V. Bowman, a special congregational meeting was held on September 10, 1900, to discuss the question, Shall we repair the old church or build a new one? When the vote was taken, thirty-eight were in favor of building a new church and thirteen in favor of repairing the old. A committee of four was appointed (Aaron Carlson, John Olson, A.G. Erickson, and August Anderson) for

the purpose of looking at lots at Central and 18th Avenue and at Central and 18½ Avenue which were up for sale. Forty votes were cast in favor of 18½ Avenue and four in favor of 18th Avenue. Through the assistance of an old-time resident and realtor in Northeast, P.C. Deming, the two lots at 18½ Avenue and Central were purchased for $1,500, with an existing house on the property that sold for $365.[10] One cannot underestimate the role of Pastor Bowman and his leadership in the story that follows. Church minutes do not indicate that the style of building was ever discussed. One can only infer from the Skogsbergh influence in the building of the Swedish Tabernacle in Minneapolis, and the new and more elaborate design of the Tabernacle in St. Paul, that such an architectural design for the new building on Central Avenue was a foregone conclusion.[11]

What Is a Tabernacle?

That question was addressed by Pastor Hjalmar Sundquist at the dedication of the Swedish Tabernacle at St. Paul on May 16, 1902. No finer definition could be given of Salem's new place of meeting.

> We propose to call this new house of worship "The Tabernacle" and we do so for two good reasons. In the first place it will consistently remind us that we have no abiding city here and should not be over-satisfied with ourselves and our new church. A congregation as well as the individual Christian, is in constant danger to forget that, especially when the temporal conditions have become somewhat improved, and all are delighted with the new church home and may be even a little proud of it—then we want to remember, that after all this is only a tabernacle—a tent of meeting for our convenience as long as we are on the journey to the true eternal temple of God. That is the original meaning of the word tabernacle. But in later years the word has been popularly applied to signify any plain and roomy building erected and used for the preaching of the gospel with the absence of strict ecclesiastical forms and ceremonies. And since this definition seems to come nearer the ideals and practices of our congregation than anything else, we have concluded to call our new church home "The Tabernacle."[12]

"Plain and Roomy"

The transition from a mission house "simple and plain" to a tabernacle "plain and roomy" becomes evident in the proposed space for worship and the preaching of the gospel. In October 1900 the building committee was directed to submit plans for a new church that would have seating for not less than a thousand and not more than twelve hundred. With a membership of only 178 at the time, this was truly a bold, visionary directive. Actually, the final plans allowed for a structure sixty-five by seventy-five feet with seating for nine hundred persons. The congregation also determined that it should be built of brick. It would not be a mission house!

If the style of the building was not a matter for congregational discussion, seating in the new building most certainly was. Some were in favor of pews, while others preferred opera chairs. Opera chairs won by a scant vote of four! Nearly seventy years later the same question would return, with church pews the winner. There was no doubt in anyone's mind, however, that the sacred space was to be organized around preaching in the midst of a responding crowd of listeners—one voice taking the authority

to speak the word of God as if God were speaking. Karl Olsson speaks of the Mission Friends' place of meeting as not a temple but "a listening post," where people assembled to hear God speak in song and word and to see God act in the salvation of souls.[13]

It was clear by how the space was organized that the place of meeting was to be musical—music by a choir was important to the meeting and its central purposes. Many memories and stories still cluster around the choir loft surrounding the preacher. The song would support the texts for preaching. In time to come there would also be, in keeping with ancient practice, a table set beneath the pulpit breaking the single focus, and to one side a bowl or font for washing. These too were holy things serving the word and celebrating the Presence.

"Smiles and Singing"

Matching the vision for the new meeting house was the joy of working together. Pastor C.V. Bowman's description of the building committee was that "they worked like a well-oiled machine," and of the members, that they "put their shoulders under the burden and helped, with smiles and singing."

> It was a pleasure to see the willingness with which all the members helped. Both the preacher and the secretary worked at times on the building as did all men in the congregation, even outsiders thought it was good fun to enter the group and work. When it was nearing completion, about twenty men used to come from their jobs to help in the church for an hour or two before the evening lowered its dark veil over us and the project. Sometimes the women came to serve coffee and good things to eat. Before we went home we would sing a verse of song and thank God. I have never had more pleasant working companions, and others felt the same way.[14]

The joy of working together was matched by the evident spirit of sacrifice. The cost of the building was $16,784.79, and the goal of the congregation was to dedicate the new building without debt. This would not be

done, however, at the expense of turning the pastor from his spiritual vocation into a fund-raiser, nor resorting to begging money from outsiders; they would bear the burden themselves.

Through subscription lists and pledges, the tabernacle was dedicated debt-free on October 6, 1901, in "a great and glorious celebration." The guest preacher for the occasion was the first president of the Covenant, Pastor C.A. Bjork, and to his surprise a special thank offering was received—not for the building fund, but for Covenant missions! Debt-free, yet always a debtor to God, the gospel, and others! That's the story of how the work began at 18½ Avenue and Central.

A Touching Footnote

Throughout the years in the mission house on Jefferson Street, care for the poor within the immigrant community was a continual concern. Shortly before moving into the new church, a question was raised with regard to helping Wendla Klarstrom, a widow in need of housing. The decision was made to purchase property at 1817 E Street Northeast (now Cleveland) and build a little house for her using some of the material left over from building the church. A forerunner of Habitat for Humanity! Following the dedication, a thank-you letter was read from Mrs. Klarstrom, extending her heartiest thanks to the church board and all the members for "the large showing of love to her by the congregation in the building of a house for her to live in. Also, her prayer to God . . . that he will crown the congregation with a great future and continuing rich blessings."[15] Older members recall that Mrs. Klarstrom frequently gave away flowers on a Sunday morning—but always to the boys (she had lost two sons) and the men!

These odd bits and pieces of memory are the fragments which make ordinary places sacred. It is what makes history so important in knowing who we are as people of God and as persons in search of our identity. In revisiting the past, hope for the future is born.

3

From Tabernacle to Church

Things That Remain

Though the spired red brick building at 18½ and Central Avenues was not commonly referred to as "the Tabernacle," as similar meeting houses in Minneapolis and St. Paul were called, it nevertheless was just that: "only a tabernacle—a tent of meeting for our convenience as long as we are on the journey to the true and eternal temple of God." Such places, however cherished, are still places on whose walls is written the word *temporary*.

Yet despite the fact that we have here no abiding city, the recollections remain. With a strain of nostalgia for the building on Central Avenue which housed so many memories, Ruth Andersson wrote a piece upon leaving the place which would resonate in many who had worshiped there:

"I wish these walls could talk," she said
— and started my reverie.
"These walls" of my Salem Church.
Sixty-nine years since they first shouldered
a protecting, steeple-crowned roof.
They have so much, so much to tell . . . of her people,
of her visitors . . .
a whole history! . . .
Home.
The House of my God.

Sheltering Walls . . .
These walls of our Salem Church,
Once attuned to another language,
To the voices and words of pastors, who in their turn
shepherded us;
loved and labored and led us . . .
praying that we learn, and grow, and serve.
For each one, these walls talk of special memories.
All they have encompassed in our lives made us the richer.[1]

Those who are now active in leadership roles at Salem and who were young people then also have a treasure-trove of memories—touched often by nostalgia and humor, but always with gratitude. Here are some of the fragments that remain:

- A recollection of Salem as a "comfort zone" in one's youth.[2]
- Memories as a boy of the clock in the sanctuary, and the significance of five minutes to twelve on Sunday mornings.[3]
- The same boy remembering the dedication of Vivian Chinander and Verna Lundgren, thinking "what a really neat thing" it was that two women from our own church were going to Africa as missionaries.
- A family feeling in being able to see everybody because they sat in the same places.[4]
- Dignified little Mr. Merrick, the undertaker, wearing a goatee, coming to church in his hack drawn by two horses.[5]
- The long stairways up to the sanctuary and the frightening memory of a young pallbearer trying to negotiate, with others, the steep descent.[6]
- Sunday School teachers who did a great job in influencing young lives.[7]
- The beginning hour of Sunday school in the sanctuary, where all ages and classes gathered to sing such songs as "In My Heart There Rings a Melody" and "Standing on the Promises."[8]
- Teachers like Vi Johnson and Iris Anderson saying many times over, "Girls, there is nothing more important than following Jesus in your life."[9]

- Sunday school Christmas programs, and afterwards going down to the basement to receive from the teacher a candy box with a string on it, filled with ribbon, red raspberry, striped peppermint, and green or orange sugar pillow candies.[10]
- A pastor forgetting to see that there was water in the baptismal font, and rescuing the occasion by inviting a family member to pray while he went for the water glass in the pulpit.[11]
- The serenity and holiness of our communion services. One member recalling her father, dressed in his best blue serge suit, serving communion and murmuring Bible verses to the receivers.[12]
- Wednesday evening prayer meetings, and kneeling on the wooden floor with elbows on the old wooden chairs, looking through the back spokes to the row behind, seeing and hearing voices of Peter Larson, Andrew Magnuson, C.H. Kjellberg, Henry Gustafson, and others praying in Swedish and English.[13]
- A real "hive" of buzzing two-, three-, and four-year-olds in that special Sunday school room called the "beehive," and listening to them sing while marching up with their offerings: "Dropping, dropping, dropping, hear the pennies fall, every one for Jesus, He will get them all."[14]
- A pastor's farewell during which the chairman announced the wrong number in the hymnal, and the hymn turned out to be "O Happy Day."[15]

Things That Change

Salem's second relocation, from Central Avenue to Silver Lake Road, is the story of a people struggling with its mission. Unlike the first move, from Jefferson Street to Central Avenue, consensus on whether to move or stay was much slower in coming and not altogether unanimous when the decision was finally made. Serious-minded people differed in their understanding of what faithfulness to the mission of the church required.[16]

Any telling of the story needs to listen to the reservations and objections voiced in the debate, as well as the reasons for change:

- Does not the flight to the suburbs leave the mission at 18½ and

Central Avenue unfinished?
- Are not the examples of commitment to Northeast by churches like Elim Baptist and Emmanuel Lutheran worthy models for Salem to follow in adapting to community needs?
- Rather than removing Salem's witness from Northeast, may not faithfulness to the mission require the congregation to remain on Central Avenue and start a mission work in one of the suburbs—which is how First Covenant planted our church in the first place?
- Will "the beloved community" ever be quite the same? The strong pull of nostalgia for the place itself and the memories associated with it, making the place sacred, must have been present in the minds and hearts of those on both sides of the issue.[17]

The question of relocation was sparked by the report of a five-year plan (1961-1965) prepared by a long-range planning committee. Included in this report was the following statement regarding membership: "Since 1935 our church membership has increased from 461 to 576 members, a 25% total increase over a 25 year period or an average increase of 5 members per year for an average yearly increase of 1%."

Following this report, a slow, gradual process began that would take many years. The reasons for change in location were several:

- No growth. Despite new membership goals set by the committee, projecting a membership of 770 by 1966, the goal turned out to be overly optimistic, with little or no actual growth.

- A transient community surrounding the church. Despite careful efforts to make overtures to community people, Sunday school attendance showed a significant decline.[18]
- A movement by a number of members out of Northeast to the northern and eastern suburbs.
- Lack of space for a full youth program.
- Lack of adequate parking for worship and other church activities.
- A building badly in need of repair, requiring a substantial amount of upgrading.

Winds of Change

In the midst of endless hours of discussion, piles of paperwork in the form of congregational letters and feasibility studies, sermons and prayers, and honest debate on mission and what faithfulness requires, the winds of change were blowing. In the many-layered story that unfolds, several key dates stand out as significant if not crucial:

- November 7, 1963. After exploring the possibilities of a group of men forming a non-profit organization to buy land and hold it for the church in case they would ever want it, a proposal that the church purchase property on 33rd and 34th avenues and Stinson Boulevard was defeated.
- June 30, 1964. A second proposal, that the congregation purchase the "Billman property," which was a horse farm just under nine acres located on the west side of Silver Lake Road south of Fifth Street NW for the sum of $75,000, was approved.
- May 26, 1965. As a result of a survey committee and an evangelism study committee, a historic decision was made: 1) that the Salem Covenant Church begin a relocation project to the Silver Lake Road property; and 2) that the congregation authorize the Executive Board to appoint a representative Building Council, subject to the approval of the General Board of the church, and that the Building Council be authorized to recommend an architect to the congregation and to

implement a financial program that would make relocation and building possible. The vote by closed ballot carried (174 yes and 79 no).[19]

- November 17, 1965. A new Executive Building Council was formed and held its first meeting.[20]
- July 12, 1966. At an Executive Building Council meeting the Plans and Construction Committee recommended the firm of Ekberg-Petri, Inc. This recommendation was approved by the council and by the congregation on July 27.
- November 28, 1967. After considerable discussion by subcommittees of the Building Council, and suggestions submitted by members of the congregation, the plan of Ekberg-Petri was approved by an overwhelming vote. Suggestions for the style of the building ranged from colonial to gothic to contemporary, which was the style finally accepted. The seating capacity of the sanctuary was discussed at great length, along with the arrangement of the worship space and whether seating would be in opera chairs or pews. Ella Roggeman, with her Norwegian persistence, expressed strong sentiment that the sanctuary should be sloped for the sake of visibility—and she won her point!
- January 28, 1968. The burning of the mortgage on the Silver Lake property at the Sunday morning service.
- November 7, 1968. A special congregational meeting was called to act upon the recommendations of the Executive Building Council to accept the new master plan that proposed, in its first phase, a sanctuary seating 504 and a choir loft seating 47; the building would include administrative offices and Christian education facilities, at a total cost of $946,000. The recommendation was passed almost unanimously. A historic meeting.
- September 28, 1969. Ground-breaking ceremonies for the new Salem Covenant Church.
- May 15, 1970. A final settlement with the Housing and Redevelopment Authority of Minneapolis for the church property on Central Avenue for $270,000.[21]
- December 6, 1970. On the Second Sunday in Advent, worship was held for the first time in the new sanctuary.

- April 4, 1971. Dedication services were held with Milton B. Engebretson, president of the Evangelical Covenant Church, as guest preacher.

Two Windfalls

Developing congregational consensus to relocate was undoubtedly shaped by two factors. One was the building itself, badly in need of repairs, with limited space for teaching and youth activities and with inadequate parking.[22] Then on Friday night, June 30, 1967, something dramatic occurred: A violent windstorm did extensive damage to the steeple. One member recalls the story like this:

> I received a call from Al Peterson, who said, "Can you come down to church? We've got a problem. Come quick!" I went down there and found that the steeple had been twisted by the windstorm and had showered bricks all over the street. It's just a wonder that nobody was injured or killed by all those bricks falling down on the sidewalk. Of course we had to proceed immediately to barricade the sidewalk as a safety precaution in case more bricks might fall from the tower, and church services were canceled for the next day.
>
> So they leaned on me to get the thing down. Later the fellows from the crane company picked me up, with another fellow; they pulled us way up on the crane to the top of the steeple, where we proceeded to remove the cross and brought it down. Then the rest of the crew took over and took down the whole tower, capping it off at the lower level. This event took place during the time there was still some uncertainty regarding our move, and it was like a message: Does it take falling bricks to move us?[23]

The other factor forming consensus was a windfall of another kind. Here is the story told by another member:

> In June of 1969 Harold Lundeen and I had returned from a fishing trip in Canada. The next morning, my secretary informed me of a telephone call from Palmer Hermundslie indicating that he wanted to make a contribution to Salem's building program. [Palmer

Hermundslie was one of the founders of Medtronics Incorporated and had attended Sunday school at Salem when he was a small boy.] I was quite surprised and also very pleased to receive such a call, and so, of course, I made the return call my first priority of the day.

Fortunately, I was able to make contact with him on the first try.

After a few idle comments relating to the results of our fishing expedition and all the big ones that got away, I said, "I understand that you called during my absence and indicated you were planning to make a gift to our church building project." "Yes," he replied, "we do wish to make a gift. If you and your pastor could come to our home, we would like you to bring your building program brochure so we can review it as a family." "Unfortunately, Rev. Stohlberg is in Chicago attending the Covenant Annual Meeting and will not return for four or five days, but we will certainly be happy to come and visit you as soon as he returns."

Upon hearing this, Mr. Hermundslie said, "Well, in the meantime maybe you would like to know the amount of our gift." My instant thought was, boy! Maybe this gift could be as much as a thousand dollars or more. "I have a check here for $101,000." Wanting to be sure I had heard correctly, I responded, "Palmer, did you say $101,000?" And the reply was, "Yes, that is correct." I exclaimed, "That's wonderful news! Now we will be able to excavate the area beneath the Fellowship Hall, which had been planned for our youth area but has been in question because of insufficient funds." There was a pause in the conversation at this point. Then Mr. Hermundslie said, "God moves in mysterious ways."

Later that morning he called again, seemingly sensing we might be somewhat apprehensive because of not having yet received the check. He invited me to bring the building brochure to their home that afternoon. His wife and their son and daughter would be there as well, since this was really a gift from the Hermundslie family, and I could pick up the check at that time. Needless to say, I was pleased to comply with this invitation. I visited with the Hermundslie family that afternoon and accepted the check from them. I was also able to reach Pastor Stohlberg in Chicago that afternoon to give him the good news. At a church business meeting the next evening, I told the congregation about this timely and generous gift which had come to us so unexpectedly.

The sequel to the story is that Mr. Hermundslie had a serious diabetic condition and was gradually losing his eyesight. He passed away less than two years later, but, unknown to us, he had included Salem Church in his will. The total amount of his gift amounted to approximately one quarter of a million dollars. So now we have the Hermundslie Lounge, which has been dedicated in honor of a man who had a vision of the future of God's work at Salem. Yes, God does move in mysterious and miraculous ways![24]

Go Forward

Much more remains to be said about the building on Silver Lake Road, and how it opened up new doors of ministry in a style quite different from that on Central Avenue. While the church's indebtedness to lay leadership[25] and the sacrificial support of many members must surely be noted, one cannot overlook the role of pastoral leadership. When one considers the work on Jefferson Street and what brought it to fruition, one thinks of Rev. E. August Skogsbergh, whose appearance was once described as "a captain on the bridge of his ship."[26] Likewise, the description fits so well the pastoral leadership of Rev. Carl Victor Bowman in bringing to pass the building on Central Avenue. And little doubt remains among those who were there that Rev. Paul E. Stohlberg also stood as captain on the bridge in steering the course to Silver Lake Road, giving his "last full measure of devotion." In concluding his final pastoral report he said, "Love God and then listen to him and see if he does not say to us, his people, GO FORWARD—march into the future with faith, with hope, and with love."[27]

4

A Story of Caretakers

Social Revolution

In nineteenth century Swedish society, the surge toward democracy along with the revival movement saw the laity coming into their own. In the conventicle or house meeting, a lay person could rise and lead a gathering of believers in prayer. Lay persons spoke to neighbors concerning matters of the heart. Many colporteurs who were sent out to distribute tracts, books, and Bibles also became lay preachers of great talent and effectiveness. Universal literacy gave people access to the Bible and other sources of spiritual edification, germinating the seed of folk leadership that the church through its parish priest system could never achieve. As a result of the revival movement, lay people became active in forming labor unions, temperance and mission societies. The notion of the priesthood of all believers—the roots of which may be traced to Luther and a century later to Philip Jacob Spener—thus became enacted in another social revolution.

Struggle for Survival

Salem's early history is the story of an immigrant people engaged in a struggle for survival in the new world. Ole Rölvaag speaks of the role of the church in aiding survival:

> It is impossible for one who hasn't seen it to imagine how the church has followed in the footsteps of the pioneer—following him through

> struggle and suffering into the wilderness, into the forest, and out over the endless prairie; how the church, like a mother, has taken him by the hand, asked him to straighten his back, rest a moment and look upward. The back was straightened, the head became more erect too, and the eye received visions of glory from above. For the early pioneers, there was no force other than the church which could draw mind and thought away from the struggle for survival. It is miraculous how it has been able to open the hearts of the people. Truly, it is a hard battle for flesh and blood to give and give and give again—and then to borrow money so as to have something to give—when one has labored so hard to scrape together a few pennies. It is enough to make one's own selfish nature burn and smart in agony.[1]

There were no safety nets such as Social Security, Medicare, or any other welfare entitlement programs. Nor was there easy access into the social life of the American community. They were resident aliens who had become outsiders to the people they had left and were still outsiders among the people to whom they had come. How the church was able not only to provide the means of drawing mind and thought away from the struggle for survival, but also to give aid and support in that struggle, is an engaging story.

People on the Margins

Despite their own poverty and lack of social status, the people of the revival—and Mission Friends in particular—were richly endowed with gifts of biblical knowledge and folk leadership to exercise both a practical and a spiritual priesthood in caring for the sick and poor among them. Early minutes of congregational meetings reveal this priestly care and how the struggle for survival shaped the mission. One could only wish to know the stories behind the names. Here are a few samplings:

- April 1889. A decision was made to take a collection to help the widow Dahlgren with the payment of her house rent.
- May 1889. A decision was made to take a collection to benefit Brother Rysell. This amounted to $13.80.
- March 1893. Reverend K.A. Isaakson had made a request through

the chairman to come and preach and receive a collection for a sick and poor family in Buffalo. His request was granted.

- March 1894. Charles L. Person raised a question as to what would be the best way to bring in money for the poor. After a period of discussion it was decided to have a song fest with a ten cent entrance donation, with the proceeds going to the poor.
- September 1894. John Olson on Marshall Street raised a question as to whether the church could do something to help a poor woman of his acquaintance go to Sweden. The question went to discussion and the decision was made to take a collection for her benefit.
- August 1896. A decision was made to gather money, food, and clothes for the poor among us, to be distributed the morning of Thanksgiving Day.
- August 1898. A motion was made that the congregation assume Brother Hedman's hospital expenses and support the subscription list already begun for him.
- June 1898. Brother Aaron Carlson reported that Emil Hedman had received $23.00 and a ticket to Gothenburg, Sweden. A total of $51.50 had come in through subscription for him.
- August 1898. The congregation urged a visit to brother Aaron Carlson as soon as possible to contribute to the help of the poor.
- April 1899. Subscription for G. Olson funeral, $40.60. One casket, $10.00.
- June 1899. A motion was made to take a collection for the benefit of Erik Nilson to help him obtain a pair of cork legs. He lay in the city hospital with both legs broken.
- September 1899. A motion was made that Andrew J. Rosen be directed to raise funds through the subscription list to pay for the funeral expenses of Mr. Klark.

A Strategy for Care

From the earliest days, the parish was divided into three geographical districts.[2] The exact boundaries of these districts are unknown, so assumptions must be made. The location of the railroad tracks crossing Jefferson Street, with no railroad bridges existing at that time, was most likely one factor. There was the Central District, which included members in close proximity to the church. The Maple Hill District was the vicinity near Maple Hill Park, formerly a cemetery and today called Beltrami Park. The New Boston District was adjacent to Central Avenue (Harrison Street at that time) from 18th Avenue to 27th Avenue. It was called New Boston because of the many early settlers in Northeast who came from Boston, Massachusetts.

Each of the three districts had a lay leader in charge. The purpose of these district meetings was to provide more intentional care for the physical and spiritual needs of members facing all the emotional and economic strains of displacement belonging to life in the new world. It was practicing accountability to and for one another in the spirit of the conventicle—with lay people in charge!

Enter Aaron Carlson

The procession of lay persons making and shaping Salem's story is long and impressive, extending from the first chairman, A.G. Erickson, down to the present.[3] In any final reckoning, the story of one person could not be told apart from the stories of many others—the interesting and ubiquitous J.K. Merricks,[4] or a Peter Larson, Leif Hermstad, Mrs. Eng

Olson, Henry Gustafson, Harlan Erickson, Vi and Elmer Johnson, Ella Roggeman, or Vera Jernall—not to mention those living caretakers of the mission in the current roster of Salem's membership.

The story of Aaron Carlson needs telling, however, if only because of his influence in the life of the congregation, the business community, and the denomination. One of six children, Aaron Carlson was born in Västra Fågelvik, Värmland, Sweden, to Carl and Maria (Olson) Anderson on January 28, 1857. He received his early education in the public schools of his parish and was confirmed in the state Lutheran church. Inheriting the mechanical skills of blacksmith and carpenter from both of his grandfathers, Aaron became a carpenter's apprentice. On April 14, 1882, at the age of twenty-five, he sailed from Oslo (then Kristiana), Norway, to New York; his destination was Minneapolis.

After working in the north woods during two winters, Aaron had the good fortune of meeting the well-known lumber merchant and president of the First National Bank of Minneapolis, Captain John Martin.[5] Recognizing the skills of this talented, hard-working young immigrant, Martin commissioned Aaron to build a wooden boat for use on a nearby lake. So impressed was Martin by his skill and craftsmanship that he got Aaron started in business. In less than ten years from his arrival in America, Aaron went into business for himself, opening a small shop that employed six men. With a specialty in interior finishing, his business grew until he was employing as many as a hundred men, most of them Swedish immigrants.[6]

The first mention of Aaron Carlson appears in congregational minutes for December 2, 1895, where thanks were expressed to him for a Thanksgiving Day offering for the poor. A few months later, on March 3, 1896, he was accepted into membership and became an active lay person. Not long after, he was chosen to serve as a member of the building committee for the new church on Central Avenue. His willingness to pay his own expenses at the annual meetings of the Covenant and the Northwest Conference gave him voice and influence beyond the local congregation. In addition to positions of leadership at Salem, he served as a trustee of the denomination, a member of the first school board of Minnehaha Academy and a successful fund-raiser for the school, and trustee and president of *Veckobladet,* a popular Swedish paper published in Minneapolis. He also occupied several positions of trust in both business and charitable organizations within the community.

Aaron Carlson's association with Turtle Lake began in 1901, when he bought and renovated an abandoned farmhouse and built two cottages alongside it for the use of pastors and other guests. Turtle Lake became a meeting place for pastors and later the Carlsons' permanent place of resi-

dence.[7] In 1928 Aaron and Minnie graciously offered their fine home on Hayes Street and 23rd Avenue, across from Windom Park in Northeast, as a home for the aged. It was dedicated in September of 1929 as "a resort for older pilgrims," Bethany Covenant Home. Freda Croner Klinka served as its first matron. In 1960 the old Carlson home was demolished to make room for a more spacious nursing and residence facility.

One's impression of Aaron Carlson, formed by his many accomplishments and the memories of those who knew him, is of a dignified, portly man in a black frock coat, starched wing-tip collar, and gold-rimmed glasses, a man always mindful of his immigrant origins and somewhat shy and diffident about his success. In his memoirs, Pastor C.V. Bowman speaks of Aaron Carlson's "indomitable will and ability to see progress clearly even when it was difficult."[8] Without such qualities in lay leadership, Salem's story would have been much different. He asked much and gave much! And there is no doubt that the church also contributed much to his early struggle for survival as a young immigrant, and to his later success as a businessman.

The Care of Souls

Through the years on Central Avenue, the Poor Fund (later called the Help Treasury) continued as an important part of the church's mission. Minutes from the deacon board in the 1920s and early 1930s reflect the needs arising from the Great Depression. The winter months record tons and tons of coal given to the poor, along with clothing and even streetcar fare so that a woman could make daily visits to a desperately ill husband in Swedish Hospital.

In addition to meeting physical needs, the church also provided for the spiritual care of members, as the minutes show. Church membership was

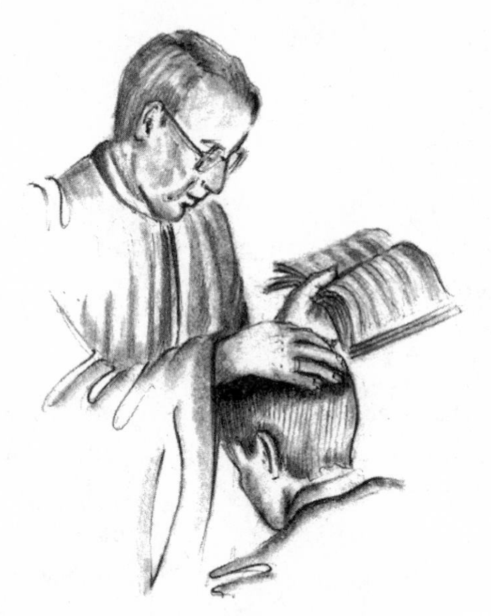

taken with utmost seriousness, measured by confessing a living, personal faith, walking in love with one's neighbors, and living a godly life. While pastoral leadership was respected and often sought, the caretakers were the laity, including the deacons and the "congregation sisters" (later called deaconesses). The spiritual priesthood of believers was not only a doctrine, but a way of life. And one should not be surprised by their passion, as Pietists, for consistency in a manner of life that was consonant with the life of Christ recorded in Scripture. There must be a congruence between what is professed and what is practiced, a congruity which could be seen both in the lives of persons and in the congregation.

Two recurring themes marked the diaconate meetings. First, the brothers always knelt for prayer at the meetings. Second, the agenda concerned the meeting of people-needs and the making of assignments for visits to those needing spiritual care.

- December 1922. Brother Livgard stated that two of our choir boys had gone up to the bowling alley on Central Avenue after church on Sunday night and smoked cigarettes. After the discussion, Brother Livgard was requested to talk to these boys personally and ask them kindly to refrain from going to this place.
- December 1922 (a week later). Brother Livgard reported that he had talked with the two boys who had gone to the bowling hall after church; they were sorry they had gone there and would refrain from going there after this.
- April 1921. Mrs. Ida Peterson was discussed, as it appeared she was leaning toward the Holy Jumpers. Mr. S.O. Livgard was requested to talk with her and report her intentions with regard to the church.
- June 1927. Brother Nels Cannon and Brother Peter Larson were asked to go see Mrs. Ida Dahlgren, who, it was reported, was attending shows.
- March 1931. Discussion of whether it was possible to have a biograph (moving pictures) in connection with a lecture in the church. It was decided that it was improper.
- June 1927. As there had been several complaints received in regard to choir members talking while in the choir seats, Brother John Gustafson was asked to instruct Mr. Reuben N. Lundstrom (the choir director) to advise the choir members to kindly refrain from talking or whispering while in the choir loft.
- April 1923. Miss Sophia Soderstrom was discussed. She had been

accepted at the regular meeting for taking in members, but had not as yet been to the Lord's Supper to be welcomed into the church. Brother Wahlstrom and Brother Charles Lundberg were instructed to go to see her and find out if she was still a Christian and, if so, why she did not attend church.

- December 1925. In view of the assertion made by Mr. __________ against Mr. ____________, it was decided to have them come before the church board as a whole and have Mr. ____________ ask Mr. ____________'s forgiveness for calling him a liar.

The Care of Souls Revisited

In the culture of the 1990s, where our sense of community appears so fragile and tenuous, such stories provide moving glimpses of a caretaking which now seems rare. No one could remain anonymous or alone with his or her failure or burden. But there was also a darker side. Communal discipline could be legalistic and judgmental. The church member who enjoyed going to shows appears often in the minutes as one needing correction. Eventually, however, she left the church, as did others, including many young people who left for similar reasons.

As so frequently happens in movements like ours, the first generation which had experienced the new life in Christ as freedom and joy was followed by the second and third generations removed from the sources of the revival. Attempts to preserve the authenticity of that "first fine careless rapture" have often put frames of ethnicity and conformity around the experience. Caretaking became concerned less with love of God and one's neighbor than with trivia like wearing makeup or bobbed hair (if one sang in the choir) and going to movies. The notion of grace and unlimited forgiveness became muted and secondary. What this part of Salem's story has taught the present generation is that, in seeking our identity as people of God, we cannot legislate new life in Christ nor ask conformity to someone else's experience. Respect for where a person is on the spiritual journey is a necessary component of real caretaking—as real as a ton of coal in winter to a family shivering in the cold!

The New Immigrants

When Salem moved from Northeast to New Brighton it was inevitable, given a vital congregational life, that new forms of ministry would emerge. Caretaking still—but in ways closer to a broader spectrum of human needs. New social revolutions on the other side of the world in the 1950s presented new challenges to the churches on this side, including Salem.

On October 5, 1975, Frank Lunquist, representing the diaconate, made the following proposal to a congregational meeting:

> We, the Board of Deacons, propose that Salem Covenant Church file proper papers with the Lutheran Immigration and Social Service . . . for the purpose of sponsoring a Vietnamese refugee family of not more than five members. To set up proper committees through our Christian Life and Social Action Committee to provide for the needs of the Vietnamese family upon their arrival. These committees would organize the congregation to provide for such things as shelter, clothing, food, employment, transportation, and above all else, Christian friendship and understanding.[9]

Included in the proposal was a detailed background including estimated costs, an introduction to the Vietnamese culture, and what such sponsorship would involve in people's acceptance, understanding, and respect for a different culture and folkways. The congregation accepted the proposal, and Frank Lunquist was appointed chairperson of Salem's Vietnamese Refugee Sponsorship Committee.[10]

- Salem's first family to arrive consisted of three young men in their twenties, two brothers and a brother-in-law: Hoa Kim Huynh, Hue Phuoc Huynh, and Kim Huynh. Leaving Vietnam as boat people, they arrived at the processing center for East Asian immigrants at Fort Chaffee, Arkansas, and came to Minneapolis in December of 1975.
- Salem's second family was larger: Lan Nguyen and his wife, Oanh Tran, and their six children. After a hair-raising escape from Vietnam by air in 1974 on the day before the government in Saigon collapsed, they arrived at Fort Chaffee, Arkansas, by way of Thailand and Guam.

From there they came to Ashby, Minnesota, in July 1975, where they were sponsored by the Trinity Lutheran Church. Moving to Minneapolis a year later because of greater job opportunities, they were sponsored by Salem.

- Salem's third family was Chanh Vo, his wife, Beo Nguyen, and their four children. Escaping by boat from Vietnam, they arrived in America in 1980 by way of the Philippines. Their fifth child, David, was the first child born to one of Salem's sponsored families, with Nanette Lunquist and Betty Ann Redeske attending his birth on June 27, 1982. Sponsors of his baptism were William and Dorothy Plice along with Frank and Nanette Lunquist. David now attends Minnehaha Academy on a Salem Special Member Scholarship.

A Church Remembers

A significant number of other Vietnamese persons have become part of Salem's extended family. As with so many Swedish immigrants, the stories of new immigrants from Southeast Asia are stories of hard work, ambition to succeed, the overcoming of obstacles, and, for nearly all, remarkable achievements in both personal and familial fulfillment of the American dream. A church of immigrants, who from its beginnings knew first-hand the struggle for survival and the ways of caretaking, could not forget, pass by, nor make invisible the new immigrants entering the American scene. At the conclusion of a recent tape-recorded interview of Lan Nguyen, it was moving to hear him say, "Thank you, Salem. We are grateful for the courage and support you have given us!"[11]

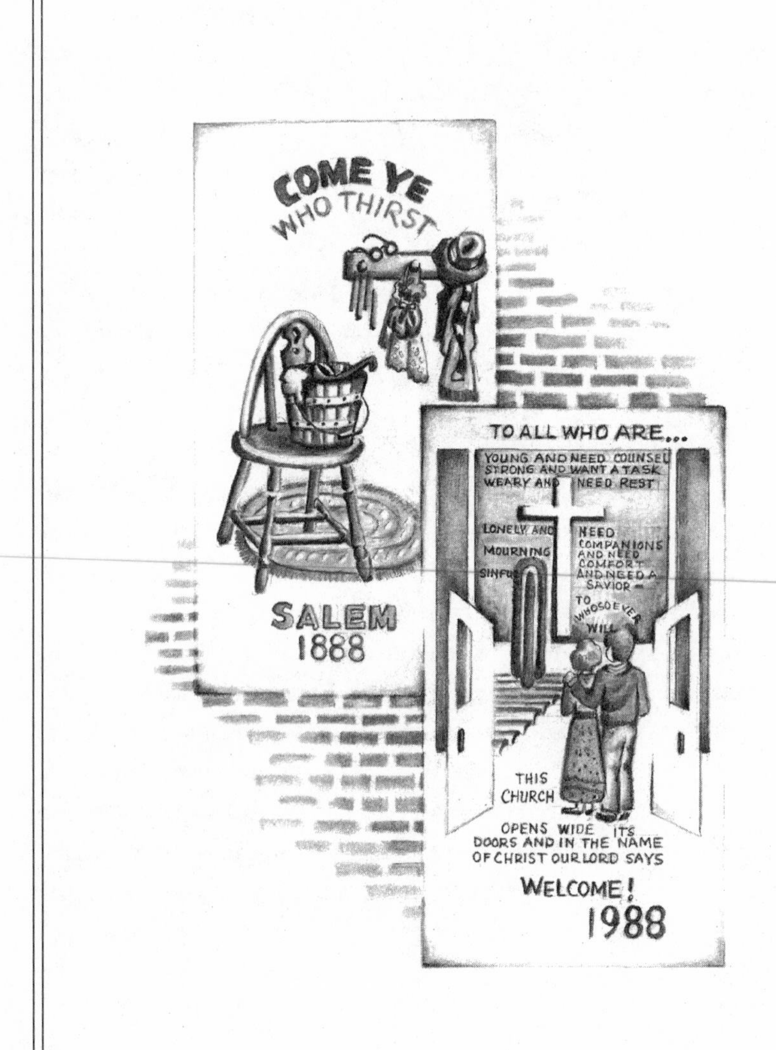
COME YE
WHO THIRST
SALEM
1888
TO ALL WHO ARE...
YOUNG AND NEED COUNSE
STRONG AND WANT A TASK
WEARY AN
NEED REST
LONELY AND
MOURNING
SINFU
NEED
COMPANIONS
AND NEED
COMFORT
AND NEED A
SAVIOR —
TO
WHOSOEVER
WIL
THIS
CHURCH
OPENS WIDE ITS
DOORS AND IN THE NAME
OF CHRIST OUR LORD SAYS
WELCOME!
1988

5

A Gospel-centered Church

"Come Ye Who Thirst"

During the year of Salem's centennial, two large, three-dimensional banners were created and mounted on the west wall of the narthex.[1] The first banner recalled memories of the water pail and dipper placed in the entryway on Jefferson Street. At the top of the banner were the words of invitation, "Come Ye Who Thirst." Beneath wooden pegs containing the remains of a former day—a scarf, a woman's hat, candles, and a pair of glasses—there was an old chair on which sat the water pail with a dipper, and the year of the church's founding: "Salem 1888."[2]

What caught one's eye in the second banner was two young people, a boy with his hand resting gently on the shoulder of a girl, standing at the open doors leading into the present sanctuary. They appear somewhat hesitant, as if strangers, seeking for whatever brought them there. But they are looking toward the suspended cross in the chancel. Above the couple are the words:

To all who are
young and need counsel
strong and want a task
weary and need rest
lonely and need companions
mourning and need comfort

sinful and need a Savior
To whosoever will . . .

Then beneath the couple are the words:

This Church
opens wide its
Doors in the Name
of Christ our Lord and says
Welcome.
Salem 1988.

Spanning a century of history with all the changes time brings, the two banners express the continuity between what the church was in its beginnings and what it would like to be now: an open, inviting fellowship of believers seeking to live and speak the gospel, the good news of God's love freely offered in Christ. Good news—not so much about things to do as about an utterly new way of understanding God, the world, and oneself, of conceiving and thus living a new, transformed life.

A Preaching Tradition

In Salem's first official history, written in 1913 by Pastor C.F. Sandstrom for the twenty-fifth anniversary, he tells a story from the early 1880s, when Swedish immigrants were flooding into the city. A revival broke out among the Mission Friends, and many were converted. During this time Rev. Emil Gustaf Törnquist, pastor of the Swedish Mission Church, was preaching one Sunday evening on the story of the Prodigal Son in Luke 15. In the midst of the sermon a woman in the gallery cried out, "I am lost! I am lost!" From the pulpit the voice of the preacher came loud and clear: "You are lost no longer, because your Father comes out to meet you."

That simple message, spoken by lay preachers, colporteurs, and converted priests who gathered in homes and later in mission houses, provided a meeting between the loving, seeking Father and the lost and hungry masses. As mentioned earlier, Rev. Törnquist was the pastor who met with the believers in the Nils Olsson home on Monroe Street in the winter of 1881.

If the continuing presence and leadership of Rev. Törnquist gave rise to a preaching tradition among Northeast Mission Friends, the arrival of his successor, Rev. E. August Skogsbergh, in 1884 certainly added a new dimension to that tradition. It was commonly acknowledged among the friends and members of the congregation that when they saw Skogsbergh's horse and carriage standing outside the meeting house on Jefferson Street, hearts beat a bit faster in anticipation of the rich gospel feast which lay in store for them.

The story of the first sermon he preached upon his arrival in America makes clear what he brought and gave to the shaping of a preaching tradition that belongs to Salem's history. Because of his reputation as a young evangelist and gospel singer who had stirred whole provinces in southern Sweden, the Swedish Evangelical Lutheran Mission Association decided to call Skogsbergh to become assistant pastor to Rev. J. M. Sanngren. After months of waiting, he finally arrived on October 10, 1876, and the congregation was to see and hear him for the first time. Here is how one observer described it:

> The meeting . . . opened with the singing of Hymn 64 in the hymnal of the Swedish state church, "Blessed be the name of Jesus, and praised be he forever." After the hymn Sanngren read a psalm of thanksgiving, spoke words of welcome to his assistant, and burst into a prayer of jubilant praise.
>
> A moment later the young man stood behind the pulpit and was speaking. . . . His text and topic were the same—an echo of the hymn they had sung, a single word: Jesus. We have no account of the sermon, but "his words fell," according to one who was present, "like a soft, warm spring shower upon a thirsty field," and another said, when asked how the speaker looked, "I can't tell, because I looked at him through tears—the tears of heavenly joy."[3]

The Ineffable Mystery

Text and topic were the same: Jesus, but Jesus as he makes himself present in the text and preaching event. Though no record of sermons from the mission house on Jefferson Street has survived—and only a few indications of sermon style from the earliest years on Central Avenue—one can make certain assumptions. For one thing, the form of the sermon most often followed the form of the text itself, in a verse-by-verse exposition of Scripture. Also, the sermon would most likely be delivered extemporaneously, with little more than a few sparse notes. The text would generally come from the lectionary of the Church of Sweden. Rev. David H. Sandstrom, whose father, Rev. C. F. Sandstrom, was pastor at Salem from 1912 to 1920, provides us with a rare and important description of Sunday morning worship during his father's ministry, and of the sermon in particular:

> Father always preached from a biblical text. He usually followed selections from the New Testament as appointed by the state (Lutheran) church of Sweden to be read Sundays in church but primarily to be texts for sermons. This lectionary covered a cycle of three years, providing a Gospel and Epistle text for each Sunday. Father felt the lectionary restrained the preacher from choosing subjects and texts that suited his fancy or that of his congregation. Over the months it provided a more fully rounded Christian message.[4]

Whether from the lectionary or in a free selection of texts, one thing remains certain: Christ proclaimed in his fullness was the point of reference for interpreting the biblical text. The Bible was food and drink, the source of nourishment and identity; but even more, it was the voice of the Shepherd going ever before his own, calling them by name, leading them in and out to find pasture, ever seeking them when they strayed, restraining and disciplining them when needed. Whether in mission house, tabernacle, or church, preaching was not for the purpose of defending the Bible or setting forth opinions about it. Preaching was for a personal and communal meeting with Christ. "The Master is here and is calling for you."

In the great tradition of preaching over the centuries, this mystical meeting occurs by finding oneself, coming to oneself. When you read of the sinful woman, there *you* were with Christ. When you heard of the Pharisee in the temple, *you* stood there as a poor creature depending on your own miserable works to merit the mercy of God. When you listened

to the story of the disciples caught in the storm and Peter coming toward Jesus on the water, *you* were the one sinking in the waves as Christ reached out his hand to save you.[5]

Staying the Course

Shortly before the arrival of Skogsbergh in Minneapolis, the Swedish Mission Church (now First Covenant) "appeared besieged from without by partisan exploiters who sought to produce discord and division." By Skogsbergh's own account, revival movements always seemed to walk a fine line between the Spirit's authentic work and a tendency to degenerate into forms of fanaticism.[6]

Rev. C. V. Bowman, pastor at Salem from 1900 to 1907, spoke of voices among the Swedish people in Minneapolis around the turn of the century that "sought to produce discord and division." One of those alien voices was heard in Northeast condemning denominations, churches, and ministers while emphasizing sanctification and baptism by the Holy Spirit. He began by holding meetings in homes, where he gathered Methodists, Baptists, and Mission Friends. As more and more people were eager to hear him, he rented a hall on Central Avenue at 25th Street, filling it to capacity.

One Sunday evening the new prophet launched an attack on Pastor Bowman because of a lecture on strange spiritual movements that Bowman had delivered at a ministers' meeting. Holding the published lecture in his hand, the evangelist would read something from the lecture and then add, "So says Bowman." After reading a Bible passage that was supposed to contradict what Bowman had written, he would say, "Thus says the Lord." Then began an emotional litany of asking, "Who is right, God or Bowman?" with the people shouting, "God is right. Bowman lies!"

The climax of the meeting came when the new prophet laid prostrate on the floor, pretending to be in the Spirit, and prophesied that within three months Salem would be divided between the worldly crowd and those who had joined his own following of true believers. This, of course, did not happen. Instead, his own group dwindled and he skipped town, leaving behind unpaid debts which he had never intended to pay—and a number of wounded souls. "In this way," Bowman added, "souls forfeit their spiritual treasure to receive something they think is better."[7]

Bridging the Generation Gap

In the book celebrating Salem's fortieth anniversary, Rev. C. A. Gavert, pastor from 1920 to 1929, paid tribute to the faith of the pioneers and the good foundation they laid. But he also saw signs of change and conflict on the horizon. Until then the Swedish language had served as, in Gavert's words, "a protective wall" around the congregation, saving it from the extremes of other movements. With the use of the English language, not to mention the encroachment of an American culture, the church would become more exposed and vulnerable. Identity and mission would be at stake. But more of this later on.[8]

According to Karl A. Olsson, only a strong pulpit leadership was equipped to bridge the gap of the generations in the years of painful transition over issues of language, lifestyle, and methodologies of mission: "In this world of first-generation hostility and suspicion and second-generation rebelliousness and curiosity, the Covenant pastor had to try to make his way. He had only one real weapon: his pulpit powers. His success and his failure are related to that circumstance."[9]

Following the pastorate of C. A. Gavert, Rev. Clarence A. Nelson was called to serve as interim pastor—most likely because he seemed too young and enigmatic to be considered for permanent pastor. After all, he was

only twenty-nine years of age! However, because of the ardor and eloquence of his preaching, he was soon called to the permanent position, where he served from 1929 to 1946. Well endowed with fluency in both languages and intimately acquainted with the first generation pioneers as well as the curiosities of a younger generation, he forged in a very powerful and distinctive way Salem's preaching tradition. Paul L. Holmer, who was profoundly influenced in his youth by Nelson, paid this tribute to him:

> Nelson's preaching in those days helped to bridge the cleft that was developing in the heretofore closely knit Swedish religious community. He was evangelical and yet current with intellectual problems and trends. Early he taught us that the extremes associated with American fundamentalism were not indigenous to Covenant evangelical history. . . . Nelson's ministry led to conversion of one's life and dispositions and yet was inextricably linked with the new burgeoning America of which all of us were becoming poignantly aware.

Nelson was wary of easy answers, vulgar unanimities, and more than a little restless with settling all of the big questions. His preaching attracted large numbers. His fervor for Jesus Christ was clear, and the demand for a life of service has continued to prick the consciences of many of us ever since.[10]

Is Gospel Enough?

Standing in the gap between the generations, however, has never been easy; neither was it for Clarence Nelson. During his ministry new opportunities gave rise to work among college students—one of Nelson's continuing interests. Likewise, the young people's society took on a different hue, with more attention given to both the personal and the social issues facing youth. And not all of this was tailored to the expectations of an older generation.

On one occasion the deacons asked for a meeting with the pastor to discuss the church and its ministry to youth. For an hour or so the deacons told of their fears for the younger generation; the church was missing the mark in its ministry by not speaking out from the pulpit against dancing, smoking, and a host of other things they felt were wrong. When they had finished, Pastor Nelson asked them to return the courtesy of listening to him. He proceeded to inform them that he would do as they asked if and when it were ever possible to exhaust the riches and depth of truth found in the wonder and grace of the Lord Christ. He informed them that, before addressing the things they asked for, he would speak of his concern over fault-finding, stingy deacons, and gossipy deacons' wives. Concluding, he asked them if they could show him a finer group of young people anywhere in the Twin Cities than at Salem, reminding them of the activities of the group, its large size, and its earnest pursuit of growth in the spiritual life. Visibly moved by these strong words, one of the deacons stood up and said, "Gentlemen, we owe our pastor and God a profound apology. I move that we go to our knees and pray."[11]

With such a spirit in pastoral and lay leadership, the painful adjustments of moving from a Swedish-speaking to an English-speaking church were made with a willingness to undertake a ministry with problems of all sorts in such a way as to make the church more fully centered in the gospel. His successors owe Clarence Nelson an immense debt of gratitude for doing what the pioneers did in the beginning—breaking open new ways of telling the gospel story and doing ministry which would connect with people's needs.

A Changing Audience

One could not conclude this broad sweep of Salem's preaching tradition without referring to the pulpit ministry of Rev. Paul E. Stohlberg, who was pastor from 1959 to 1978. Though the message remained the same, the audience changed significantly in the move from Central Av-

enue to Silver Lake Road. In the changing circumstances his preaching reflected not only a serious attention to the biblical text but an interpreting of the culture as well. The topics and illustrations of his sermons were of a more popular style, while at the same time revealing a clear understanding of what Luther says constitutes true evangelical preaching: knowing the difference between law and gospel. In a sermon titled "Thou Shalt Not!—Says Who?" based on the gospel of the day, Matthew 5:17-20, he speaks of the breakdown of authority in family life and society, and interprets the Ten Commandments. Here is how the sermon ends:[12]

> To honor the Ten Commandments we do not need to cling to some picture like that which Hollywood gave us long ago when a magic arm descended from the sky to engrave the Commandments on the rock with what looked like "a celestial pneumatic drill." I hear them NOW as the Word of God and I listen again with awe to what Jesus said: "Do not suppose I am come to abolish the law. . . . I did not come to abolish but to complete it. . . ." And what is that completion? There are a number of answers but I limit myself to one. That completion is what we can become by the grace of God. Anyone who has honestly tried to live by the Commandments becomes immediately aware of one important truth: His own inadequacy to live a life of complete love for God and one's neighbor. . . .
>
> The Law shows us our need for divine forgiveness! And the Gospel tells us lawbreakers that we are forgiven and gives us grace by which we may grow daily more like Christ. It is when we honestly recognize, in the presence of the Law, that we are "debtors" and "trespassers" trusting in the grace of Christ as the only source of true goodness, that we are ready to hear the word that says, "Go in peace, thy faith hath made thee whole."

Following in Salem's preaching tradition, Paul Stohlberg led his listeners as penitents to the foot of the cross, to a personal meeting with the crucified and risen Christ.

Giving the Invitation

On January 3, 1988, the first Sunday of the centennial year at Salem, the preacher standing in the apostolic succession of those preceding him took up the same refrain, announcing again the good news, always as fresh and new as on the day it was first spoken:

> The church with the pail and dipper is still the bearer of God's invitation—good news for the thirsty. There is a meeting place with an address where you are not only welcome but where your thirst can be quenched. There is a Word. There is a font of life. There is a table. There is broken bread. There is a water pail and dipper. "In, with, and under" these earthy things is the presence of the living Christ,

God's chosen One, the Bright and Morning Star, the Lamb of God who takes away the sins of the world. The One who offers the gift of eternal life freely to all who thirst says, "Come, the gift is yours, without money and without price." There is no better menu any place. The source of life is not a concept, nor a theology, nor a ritual, nor an organization, nor even an experience however ecstatic. The source of life is a Person—Jesus, the living One who speaks and with outstretched hand says to you, "Welcome!"[13]

6

A Worshiping Church

"Reverent, Festive and Beautiful"

In 1900 the Covenant's Committee on Ritual produced an important document entitled "Guide to Christian Worship," which not only reflected concern for a living worship among congregations at the turn of the century, but continues to give wise counsel for shaping worship in Covenant churches today. The essay bears the marks of the revival movement as reaction against cold, lifeless, liturgical forms: "The Christian worship is a form for the corporate life of the church but this life must have the freedom to develop such forms as are consistent with its own nature. One cannot confine Christian church life within one for-all-time-established form. It grows freely and breaks through all coercive forms."[1] But if there is reaction here, the call for order is clear. "Spiritual life is the inner, true essence of worship but this life must reveal itself through the outward forms of words and deeds. Forms can be without life, but life cannot be without forms. . . . The outward form of worship should be reverent, festive and beautiful."[2]

With roots in both Lutheranism and classical Pietism, Covenant people knew about the priesthood of all believers not only in caretaking but in worship. "The church is not a chaotic heap of members but a body in which each member has his place and function," thus allowing for "a free participation of the attendants" in prayer, song, and personal witness. Yet good order in the body should be reflected in "the beautiful worship of the Lord" and always appear in "a worthy and gracious manner."[3] The story of Salem's worship reflects the interplay of order and freedom, or what the late dean of North Park Seminary, Glenn P. Anderson, called the "churchly and conventicle traditions."

Worship in the Mission House

Though we have no record describing what worship was like on Jefferson Street, there is little doubt about what the Covenant's earliest historian, C. M. Youngquist, says about the services of early Mission Friends:

> Singing was prominent in these services. The whole congregation would join the unaffected and beautiful songs which were willingly led by brothers and sisters who had the gift. At the conclusion of the sermon it seemed as if the singing would not end. A verse, or perhaps only a refrain, would be repeated again and again until the words were impressed upon our minds and joy stood high on the ceiling.[4]

A Trumpet or a Harp?

At the all-day business meeting of the congregation on New Year's Day 1891, the issue of a hymnbook was discussed. The two hymnbooks in question were *Evangelii Basun* (The Gospel Trumpet) and *Sionsharpan* (Zion's Harp). When the vote was taken, the congregation was evenly divided. And though the minutes contain no record of breaking the tie, *Evangelii Basun* won out, probably because of the congregation's close ties with the editor, Rev. E. August Skogsbergh.[5] Both hymnbooks, however, were quite similar in that they reflected the three main streams of revival hymnody:

- The Church of Sweden, represented by *Den Svenska Psalmboken* (The Swedish Psalmbook of 1819), mainly the work of Johan Olof Wallin, popular preacher, pastor, and later archbishop of Uppsala.
- The Pietist/Moravian hymns of the revival movement, represented by C. O. Rosenius, Oscar Ahnfelt, Lina Sandell, Nils Frykman, A.L. Skoog, and others.
- Gospel songs from the Moody and Sankey revivals of the late nineteenth century.

Which Organ?

From the beginning of worship in the meeting house, the organ had been the instrument of choice. When John K. Merricks was received into membership ten days after the organizational meeting, on December 27, 1888, he was asked to serve as organist "whenever present at the meet-

ings." Two months later Augusta Frisk (no relation to the present Frisks) was hired as organist and song leader for six dollars a month. After serving for six years, she was dismissed by the congregation because of a continual bickering over salary.

Axel Wallin, from Galesburg, Illinois, was called and served as organist and song leader for two years. He was followed by Oscar Johnson, from Cleveland, Ohio, and the salary was raised to fifteen dollars a month. During interims without an organist, Olaf Holmer was invited to take charge. The importance of the organ is best attested to by the congregation's involvement in choosing a new instrument. When the church decided to purchase a new reed organ, four organs were brought into the mission house for a trial run on June 22, 1896, like candidates running for office. The Packard organ was elected.

During 1894 two musical groups were formed—a string band and a male chorus. In his annual report on January 1, 1895, Pastor August Sjöberg took note of these two groups with the interesting comment, "Both are in their beginnings but the Lord shall ever change these gifts in his service to his Name's glory and honor. So we think and believe." It sounds as though hope for these fledgling groups rested in change for the better. One might consider Sjoberg's surprise if he had known that the string band continued for a number of years before its demise, was revived at the ninetieth anniversary of the congregation, and still flourishes today.[6]

Worship in the Tabernacle

When the congregation moved in 1901 from the mission house on Jefferson Street to the red brick tabernacle on Central Avenue, the Packard organ went with them, together with the Skogsbergh-Skoog hymnbooks, the string band, and the male chorus. The harmonious combination of the

churchly and conventicle traditions was not lost in memory, but expressed in a new setting with a clear bent toward the informal. Paul L. Holmer draws an interesting and accurate contrast between the downtown churches and Salem:

> The English citizens with money, power, prestige, and culture lived elsewhere and were the captains of industry, patrons of the symphony, arbiters of taste and university oriented. They also sustained the downtown churches where preaching seemed a bit impersonal and Bach and Palestrina gave style to sounds. Colleges and universities seemed quite far away.
>
> And Christian faith at Salem was still at home with nasal tenors, string bands, informal expression, and those strong hands and backs. Aaron Carlson's sash-and-door factory looked almost like an outpost of Salem church, for there is where many clever Swedish artisans were initially employed.[7]

A Sunday Morning Service

We are much in debt to David Sandstrom for his reminiscences of Sunday morning worship at Salem during his years of growing up under the ministry of his father, Rev. Carl F. Sandstrom, who served as pastor from 1912 to 1920. One observes the harmonious combination of good order and freedom that is characteristic of a Covenant service:

> Shortly before eleven o'clock our organist and choir leader Joseph Burns, emerged from a stairway leading up to the south gallery and walked along the front wall to his organ. Always easy and reassuring in manner, he had been brought up in the church, had taught piano to children of the parish, and later became head of the music department at Minnehaha Academy, our church-related high school. I am not certain that he played a prelude to the service. If he did, it was not for the sake of quiet; that was already there. Soon the choir entered, the women from the south door below the platform, the men from the stairway Mr. Burns had used. The choir always had some fifty voices.
>
> Then Father entered from the north room just below the platform.

He slowly closed the door behind him, glanced out at the congregation but never with a full look, mounted the platform and took the center chair. He gave no call to worship but took ample time for his own silent prayer. Then he walked to the pulpit and announced, "Let us begin worship this morning with hymn number 501." [David Sandstrom remembers this hymn in particular, which was "Sabbath Day of Rest and Cheer."]

Often we sang a second hymn. Then followed the reading of the scriptures. The selection was a psalm, a passage from one of the great prophets or from the teachings of Jesus, or a gospel narrative out of Jesus' life, or something out of the New Testament letters. Whatever the selection, it was devotional and readily understood by the worshipers. It was not necessarily correlated with Father's sermon; it stood in its own right.

Then came the pastoral prayer. I'm sure it was quite typical of the spontaneous prayers offered in nonliturgical churches. But sometimes Father added a petition in behalf of himself, *"that he who is wont to nourish others might himself be nourished."*

After prayer, came the announcements. Not having a printed calendar, Father verbally reported coming events and other points of interest. Occasionally someone, often an usher, came forward to slip Father a belated note. At times these little "afterthoughts" precipitated a bit of merriment.

When the offering had been received, the treasurer and two other trustees disappeared immediately to count the collection. You knew the offering had been well cared for when the three men reappeared and went to their places in the congregation.

The choir usually sang one anthem. Joseph Burns always had a good choir. I remember that twice the choir performed in concert parts of Handel's "The Messiah," to a packed church. For these occasions Burns obtained professional soloists. Now for the sermon. . . .[8]

Shaping a Musical Tradition

The presence of Joseph Burns, as described above, signaled a growing taste for the more classical expressions of church music. As director, pianist, organist, and composer, his influence in cultivating a musical tradition in Salem's worship cannot be underestimated. In January of 1903 Joseph E. Burns, then an active member of the Young People's Society, was asked to direct the choir and lead the singing at the regular meetings "for the time being." The "time being" lasted for twenty-two years![9]

During his tenure Burns and the choir were instrumental in purchasing and installing Salem's first pipe organ, at a cost of three thousand dollars. With a generous gift from Aaron Carlson, the organ built by George Kilgen and Son was dedicated debt-free. A dedication concert was held on February 22, 1911, with Professor J. Victor Bergquist as guest organist and Joseph Burns as director of a choir of fifty voices. Among the choral presentations was an anthem by a favorite Swedish composer, Gunnar Wennerberg, based on Psalm 114: "When Israel Out of Egypt Went"—which no doubt struck a chord in the heart of an immigrant community. An interesting footnote to the program contained these words: "Ladies are kindly requested to remove their hats," implying something about the millinery styles of that time.[10]

The hymn mentioned above that Sandstrom so fondly remembers from his youth, including even the number, came from the first official hymnal of the denomination, *Sions Basun* (Zion's Trumpet) of 1908.[11] However, an earlier hymnal, *Sions Glädjebud* (Zion's Joyous Message), was used for a time during Rev. C.V. Bowman's pastorate. In the transition from Swedish to English, the congregation on Central Avenue would use two more hymnbooks: *The Covenant Hymnal* of 1931, commonly referred to as "the brown hymnal," and *The Hymnal* of 1950, often called "the green hymnal." Each succeeding hymnal has drawn from the larger reservoirs of the church's song, but none deeper than the wells of its own heritage.

Holy Things

While the tabernacle was "the listening post" with the preaching of the word central, the mystery of holy things—the table for eating and the font for washing—would not be taken lightly. On September 9, 1937, a new communion table and baptismal font were dedicated, made of cherry wood by a skilled craftsman and member of the congregation, Richard Monson. Shortly after that, paraments for pulpit and table were added. A brass

cross and candlesticks given as a memorial created a flurry of discussion over a growing trend toward the ritualistic.[12] Nine years earlier two paintings by the artist Carl Morin had been placed in front of the sanctuary; they were among the first memorials given to the church. The painting "The Good Shepherd" was presented by the choir and male chorus in memory of Joseph Burns; the other, "Christ in Gethsemane," was given in honor of Charles G. Larson, who served for nineteen years as church chairman. The pipe organ from 1911 was restored once and remained in use until 1960, when it was replaced by an organ built by Hillgren Lane and Company.[13] This instrument would become a musical link between the tabernacle on Central Avenue and the church in New Brighton.

Worship in the New Church

Entering the worship space on Silver Lake Road for the first time must have evoked in the members a mix of feelings both of gain and loss, of wonder and surprise. What one Minnesota author described upon entering another church building might have been their experience: "The surge of vertical space, the immense upward vault. Architecture as psalm, the soul flung to the rafters in lament, in praise, in its wild reach for its Maker."[14]

A giant step from mission house and tabernacle!

But there were continuities with the past, not only in the gospel proclaimed from pulpit, table, and font, but now as it was expressed in wood, brick, stained glass, and textiles. Ruth Andersson's reverie upon leaving old Salem was followed by impressions of her initial feelings upon entering the new worship space:

> Today my new church has opened its doors,
> Three and a half miles and seven months ago, we bade farewell
>   to the home which was the only one I had known.
> Now on a Sunday I have entered the high wide doors
>   into a new community.
> The newness is everywhere to see,
> I walk the slate entry into the green-carpeted aisle,
>   to seat myself comfortably upon a black-cushioned pew.
> My sight follows the light from a single, unusual window
>   to the brown slat and brick walls, ceiled by white.
> Modern light slowly dim.
> Relentlessly, my eyes are drawn to the simplest symbol,
>   For me, it dominates this sanctuary;
>   two simple pieces of wood . . . unadorned.
> And as I worship God, the force of that cross
>   is pressed in upon my heart.
> My mind cannot comprehend it . . .
>   a body hanging there,
>   nails rending the flesh of hands and feet . . . blood . . .
> How could the straining weight of a man's body
>   be held there by so harsh a means?
> My heart is overwhelmed in grief,
>   feeling the agony of that physical pain.
> The newness about me fades . . .
>   pain that will not give . . .
>   sun and fever and blood . . .
>   hour after hour after hour.
> A cross was centered in the sanctuary of my old church home too;

Have I perhaps learned anew its deeper meaning?
The physical agony I think I can identify and feel . . .
It is but a faint hint of his agony
when the leaden load of my sin
Was added to the weight of his body . . .
upon two simple pieces of wood.
Forgive me
I pray . . . again.[15]

Holy Things Interpreted

Despite an earlier Covenant reticence to accept any visual embellishments, or what someone has called "pictorial exuberance," that might distract from the preaching of the word (the exception being so-called "edifying art," such as the Morin paintings noted above), the interior of the church on Silver Lake Road was a significant affirmation of artists and their creative offerings. At the Festival of Dedication on Palm Sunday, April 4, 1971, the order of service bore witness to that affirmation of art through a commentary on the holy things in the sanctuary. In addition to the cross and its centrality in worship, the other objects noted were these:

- The Eye Brow Window is a symbol of the Lord looking upon his people. It looks into the sanctuary, into every seeking heart and sees the longing there. It looks out upon the world—and it is a look of love and concern. . . .[16]
- The massive pulpit placed in a forward position in the sanctuary says that preaching and teaching the word of God occupies a preeminent place in the church's ministry. . . .
- The communion table in the center of the chancel is the focal point of worship and indicates that for the People of God it is the most sacred single act of worship. . . .[17]
- The font is the symbol of the sacrament of Holy Baptism. It suggests to us the centrality of the sacraments along with the word. . . .
- The prayer rail emphasizes the importance of prayer in our worship experience . . . it reminds us that prayer is both a corporate and private act of worship.

- The two burning candles are a vivid reminder that Jesus Christ is both God and man. . . .
- The organ, with its majestic and quiet tones, symbolizes the prominence of music in our worship experience. . . . Through music we "praise God from whom all blessings flow."

The program of dedication also contained an impassioned prayer for the church: "Come, Holy Spirit, Heavenly Dove, and pour out on us your power and your love. Help us to come alive! Fill us. Send us before you in service. . . ." Following the death of Pastor Paul Stohlberg in May of 1978, the family commissioned Neale Murray, of the art department of North Park College, to create a wood sculpture for the rear wall of the sanctuary.[18]

- The sculpture represents the Spirit as a descending dove who anoints us as we enter beneath it and is an unseen presence among us as we worship together. As we leave the sanctuary the Spirit also stands before us as we go forth in his name to serve the world.

An affirmation of art in the worship space also served to call forth artistic gifts within the congregation. On Sunday evening, January 20, 1980, a service of dedication took place for the unveiling of a mural in the youth room painted by Greg Carter, who was then a student in the art department of the University of Minnesota.

- The mural is in two parts. The first is an introductory passage about the creation of the world. The second is a description in images of the world as the artist saw it, containing reminders of human suffering and the wonderful surprises of grace.[19]

When an extensive remodeling of the chancel occurred in 1987 for the installation of a new pipe organ designed by Walter Holtkamp of Cleveland, Ohio, several additions followed:

- The paraments for the pulpit and table using the colors for each of the festivals and seasons of the Christian year, telling the Christ story: white for his birthing and rising again; purple for the seasons of preparation, both for his coming and for his passion and dying;

red for special days of church celebration like Pentecost, confirmation, Reformation, and church anniversaries; and green for seasons following festivals, suggesting new life and growth in the mystery of Christ as we live out the mystery.[20]

- The "fish scale banner" recalling the fishing for people to which Jesus calls disciples; the fish scales represent the individual members of the congregation reaching out to others, the downward movement accenting the preaching of the word, and the colors giving us visual reminders of the unfolding of the Christian story in the seasons of the church year.[21]
- The seven candles behind the table signifying the seven days of creation, the sevenfold Spirit promised by Isaiah, or the seven lampstands of the seven churches in the book of Revelation as reminders of the One who still lives and walks among us.

The Song Goes On

In the year celebrating Salem's centennial, the voice of the congregation in song was the voice of the early Mission Friends still singing the old Lutheran chorales, the folk songs of the revival, and gospel songs. They used *The Covenant Hymnal* of 1973 and a little blue supplement prepared for the Covenant's centennial in 1985, *Come, Let Us Praise Him*. In 1990 the Covenant Hymnal Commission produced another supplement, *The Song Goes On*, which reflects changing musical styles as well as older songs of the tradition. Since its publication Salem has used this supplement with appreciation. Lending support to congregational song was the classic voice of the new Holtkamp tracker action organ, played with consummate and professional skill by Salem's organist since September of 1976, Cindy Wobig Reents. Through the sensitive and gifted leadership of Terry Sheetz, director of the Sanctuary Choir, the centennial year closed on a celebrative note with an offering of Mendelssohn's Second Symphony by orchestra, organ, soloists, and choir, and its thematic rendering of "A Mighty Fortress Is Our God."

A Worship Open to Life

At the twenty-fifth anniversary of Salem, founding pastor E. August

Skogsbergh expressed his gladness in "the little contribution" he had made, then said that his prayer was that in the congregation's outward growth it would not lose its inner power: "For a congregation, big or small, to have a Christian reputation it must have spiritual youthfulness and freshness. . . . To grow rigid in form and church formality goes so easy. We must therefore at all times be on the watch in preserving our first love so that it not burn out or cool off."[22]

The point then and now is never to be caught in what is altogether predictable or in what comes to be ritualistic, but to be ever fresh and young "in this ancient business of the Spirit."[23]

7

Women with Names

A Man's World—Almost

On that cold winter evening of December 17, 1888, when, after due notice, a meeting was called for the purpose of organizing a congregation, the minutes record that approximately thirty "brothers" gathered. One might conclude that "brothers" was used in an inclusive sense, as in the old biblical usage of "brethren" including both men and women. But when the charter of organization was signed, the thirteen names were all men.

Another meeting was called a month later, on January 19, 1889, for the purpose of accepting new members. The minutes read like this: "Opportunity was given for those desiring entrance into the church to present themselves and to testify to God's grace and mercy in their lives. Many testimonies with glorious evidence were heard."

Whether by the secretary's whim or choice, the names of women received into membership were not used unless one was a single woman or widow. They were listed, rather, as "Charles Johnson and wife," for example. Another year would pass before it became apparent that wives also had names. Then the minutes read, "Charles Johnson and wife Carolina." The women did have names! I find it touching that in Pastor E. August Skogsbergh's greeting at the twenty-fifth anniversary of Salem, he mentions two women by name with special affection: "dear Greta" (Frans Larson's wife) and Kajsa (A.G. Erickson's wife), both wives of charter members.[1]

Leading the Way

One thing is clear: women in the mission house on Jefferson Street were not invisible. Five years before the official organization of the congregation, the women had already organized into a Sister Society. This took place in the same home on Monroe Street where the Salem story had be-

gun two years earlier in the conventicle meeting at Mrs. Nils Olsson's. The following seven women were on hand, identified by their husband's names: Mrs. Nils Olsson, Mrs. Frans Larson, Mrs. L. Lindberg, Mrs. C.W. Lunquist, Mrs. J.K. Merricks, Mrs. A.G. Ericksson, and Mrs. Erick Erickson. Their purpose was to sew for the needy and to raise funds for church auctions. They continued to have an important role in congregational life, contributing to local needs, the Bethany and Ebenezer homes, Minnehaha Academy, the Northwest Mission Association, the Sailors' Home in Boston, and missionaries in China. In April of 1931 the Sister Society changed its name to the Martha Society, after the sister in the Bethany home who showed hospitality to the Lord by her serving.

Early minutes of the Sister Society record clothes made by the group, piece by piece. Others recall shelf upon shelf of clothes in the basement of the church on Central Avenue made by the sewing circle and distributed to the poor in the community by the church missionary, Olga Gustafson.

With a continuous history in Salem since 1883, the society is still active today as the Missions Fellowship Group of Covenant Women.[2]

Shining Models

The revival movement in Sweden had broken and ploughed fallow ground in many areas of communal life, but especially in giving place to women. In the 1850s two women, Maria Nilsdotter and her close friend Britta Jonsdotter, from nearby Karlskoga in the province of Värmland, gathered other women in a conventicle around the gospel and made the remarkable discovery that because of grace they were also bound to the needs of neighbor.[3] In this case, "neighbor" meant lost children being auctioned for farm and domestic labor much as were black slaves in early America.

Appealing in vain to town and church officials, Maria, Britta, and other women in the conventicle found many of these children, bought them at auction, placed them in homes, and taught them to read and write. Their only means of support came from the circle of sisters themselves by sewing, handwork, and other marketable skills.

Out of this conventicle came a children's home, school, and Sunday school, thus laying the groundwork for what is known today as the Karlskoga Folk High School. One of Maria's sons, Carl Johan, was converted and became an outstanding lay preacher and colporteur. He also became the father of David Nyvall, one of the founders and the first president of North Park College in Chicago.[4] Maria Nilsdotter became known as *Mor i Vall* (Mother in the Valley), Vall being the farmstead on which she lived. Her homestead outside of Karlskoga draws scores of visitors each year. And all of this because Maria, a widow at the age of forty with six children of her own, was a Pietist, female, and trouble-maker whose vision for lost children upset the status quo in town and church.

A Heritage of Nations

In the spirit of *Mor i Vall*, the Sister Society on Jefferson Street led the way to new ventures in organizing women for mission on Central Avenue. On March 28, 1904, another group of seven women met at the home of Helen Peterson on Johnson Street and organized the Young Ladies'

Mission Club. Their names were Ellen Burns, Hulda Hedin, Selma Hultman, Helen Peterson, Hilda Peterson, Hulda Peterson, and Ida Wahlquist. The inspiration for the group came from hearing a missionary speak on Psalm 2:8: "Ask of me and I will make the nations your heritage, and the ends of the earth your possession." At the first meeting, Ida Wahlquist became president and the seven young women took a two-fold pledge: not to take part in worldly amusements and to pay their dues. The purpose of the group was to further the cause of missions at home and abroad. Their motto was "Never put off until tomorrow what you can do today."

A few months later Christine Matson, a woman of fragile health and the wife of the first Covenant missionary to China, Peter Matson, was invited to speak to the mission club about China. Upon leaving she promised to send the group the name of an eleven-year-old Chinese girl, Chen King U, who was in need of support. From this initial contact, the Young Ladies' Mission Club, now growing in numbers, took on the support not only of Chen King U, but also of a Chinese woman who sold Bibles and another little girl, by the name of Ting. From January of 1909 the young women's group was called the Chen King U Society, and China became their passion.[5]

The Circle Widens

What is so remarkable about the story is how this society touched the lives of so many and shaped to an even greater extent the congregation's commitment to its world mission. With Chen King U, the Martha Society, the interim pastorate from 1911 to 1912 of missionary Joel S. Johnson of Kingchow, China, and a congregation lending support, these are a few of the consequences within the church family itself:

- Esther Kjellberg Franzen (1898-1983), the oldest in a family of five, felt the missionary call in her early teens. Following her training and commissioning, she first went to Peking for language study. From Peking she traveled inland to Kingmen to teach at a girls' school. Despite famine and nationalistic propaganda which taxed the endurance of the mission staff, her first school year ended with a number of the older girls being baptized into the Christian faith. After three and a half years, illness forced Esther to return home. She arrived in Minneapolis on February 11, 1927, only to discover that her mother had been stricken with a heart attack and had died an hour before her arrival. On January 22, 1929, Esther was married in Stockholm, Sweden, to a widower, Frans Elof Franzen, a China missionary under the Swedish Covenant. They lived in Sweden from 1929 to 1932 and then returned as missionaries to China, serving for six years at Hupeh under the Swedish Covenant. Following her husband's death she returned to Chicago, where she served for some years as housemother in the nurses' dormitory at Swedish Covenant Hospital. Upon her retirement she returned to Minneapolis, where she lived for several years. She spent her last few months at Bethany Home until her death on March 10, 1983.

- Martha Joanna Anderson (1906-1948), daughter of Rev. and Mrs. Adolph Anderson, who had dedicated her in infancy to missions, was commissioned by the Covenant Annual Meeting on June 20, 1937, for missionary work in China. On a cold winter night in 1938 Martha

left from the old Union Station in Minneapolis to spend the next six and a half years as bookkeeper for the Covenant mission in Siangyang. In 1945 she spent one year of a two-year furlough at North Park, studying Bible with three of her Salem friends, Vivian Chinander, Verna Lundgren, and Elizabeth Lundeen. She returned to China in

September of 1947 to begin her second term. It was a time of political and military upheaval, causing the American consulate to advise all missionaries to leave. The mission staff made the decision to stay through Christmas, hoping the unrest would subside. The story of the events of January 7, 1948, is told below.

- Alice Jensen (1901-1992), a recent widow, desired to do something meaningful with her life and heard of the need for a bookkeeper at the Karawa station in what was then called Congo (now Zaire). She applied for the position, and the Covenant commissioned her in 1940 at the age of forty! Though called as a bookkeeper, she was soon asked to teach some girls' classes and later began work translating the scriptures into Lingala, the trade language of the country. Because older people are looked upon with reverence in the African culture, Alice's age was in her favor, and the people became very fond of her. After four terms in the Congo she returned to the States, working as a secretary in the nursing office at Swedish Covenant Hospital. Upon retirement she enrolled at North Park College to complete work for a degree, which she received in June of 1981 at the age of eighty years! Her last days were spent at Covenant Village of Northbrook, Illinois, where she died on February 26, 1992.
- Vivian Chinander (1917-) from her youth had an early interest in serving as a missionary in China. When the field in China was closed, her interests were redirected to the Congo. Vivian graduated from a cadet nursing program at the University of Minnesota, then took a year of Bible and missions orientation at North Park College and Theological Seminary. She continued her studies at the University of Minnesota, earning a nursing degree. In 1951 she and Verna Lundgren were commissioned at Salem for missionary service. For two years she worked at Karawa and Wasolo with lepers. From 1963 to 1967 she assisted Dr. Helen Bergquist in setting up a nursing school at Karawa, which was accredited in 1967 by the World Health Organization. Her last term was spent in Gbado, teaching public health courses to men and women in the Bible school. After thirty years of missionary service in Zaire, Vivian returned to the States, serving for a period of time at Swedish Covenant Hospital, then moving back to

Minneapolis and her home church, Salem. She now lives in retirement at Covenant Manor in Golden Valley.

- Verna Lundgren (1919-   ), as a young girl in Sunday school, felt a strong desire to offer her life for missionary service. This desire was reawakened at a Covenant Annual Meeting as she listened to a moving address by the missionary veteran from China, Peter Matson. Offering herself for missionary service, she was encouraged by the Covenant Board of Missions to prepare herself for teaching. She attended North Park College and the University of Minnesota, and graduated from Augustana College in Rock Island, Illinois, in 1950. After language study in Belgium, she arrived in the Congo in 1952 and served her first term in Bokado, directing the work of the schools. During her second term in Wasolo she also directed schools in that area, including the supervision of construction crews! On her third term she was on loan to the Congo Polytechnic Institute, an agricultural school, where she was secretary to the director. Because of Communist infiltration, the staff was evacuated to Leopoldville in July of 1964, and after a short time she returned home. She taught second grade in the Anoka school system for fifteen years, retiring in 1981. Verna presently resides at the Augustana Home in Minneapolis.
- Elizabeth Lundeen (1919-   ), as a high school student, felt called to go to China as a missionary. When the field in China closed, she served

in the Philippines and Japan in the Army Nurse Corps. Upon returning home she took the one-year missionary orientation course at North Park. While in Chicago she met Virginia Ohlson. Through her encouragement and help Elizabeth received an assignment with the Occupation Forces in Japan, where she worked for four years in the areas of nursing and midwifery. Returning home in 1956 following a year in Okinawa, she served for four years under the Southern Presbyterian Board, where she was director of nursing at the Hodokowa Christian Hospital in Osaka. In 1960 Elizabeth returned to the States to work as a school nurse for Public Health of Minneapolis. At the Annual Meeting of the Covenant in June 1989 she was honored with the Theodore W. Anderson Award as the outstanding Covenant lay person of the year. She resides in her home in Minneapolis.

- Anna Marie Kylander Oudal (1935-) also felt the call to ministry in her youth, and eventually entered North Park Seminary. During her studies she learned of a teaching position open at the Covenant school in Unalakleet, Alaska, and she was called to fill that position in August of 1960. While there she met a young man on the staff from First Covenant Church in Minneapolis, and in May of 1962 she and Willmar (Bill) Oudal were married in the church at Unalakleet. Bill taught mathematics, biology, and other related subjects, as well as coaching the basketball team and directing the school choir. Anna Marie taught English, history, and piano. Both served as dorm parents to the resident students. Because of rising costs, the Covenant was forced to close the high school in the summer of 1985. The Oudals then moved to Glenellen, Alaska, where Bill is serving as principal of the high school and Anna Marie is a substitute teacher. The Oudals have four daughters,
- In addition to those called to missionary service from within the Salem family, mention must also be made of the significant contributions made by these two women's societies toward the support in 1915 of Rev. and Mrs. Joel Johnson ("with help from Aaron Carlson"), and in 1934 of Dr. and Mrs. Barton Nelson, medical missionaries stationed at Bethesda Hospital in Siangyang, China. This support con-

tinued from 1934 to 1942, when ill health forced the Nelsons to return to Minneapolis. The China passion has always been strong at Salem!

A Martyr Strain

During the observances of the centennial year, three stained glass panels illumined by natural light in the fellowship hall were dedicated. The central panel is the cross and crown symbol from the rose window in the sanctuary on Central Avenue. The panel hanging to the left contains a sheaf of wheat, suggesting thanksgiving for harvest and bread for the Eucharist, appropriate for remembering those known and unknown saints through whose labors we have entered. The panel to the right was dedicated with these words:

> This panel affords Salem the opportunity of memorializing one of its own members who in 1948 became a martyr for Christ, Martha Anderson, missionary to China. The appropriate symbol of a chalice with grapes is another recognized symbol of the Eucharist, suggesting thanksgiving for the fruit of the vine bruised and crushed so that life and salvation might be offered to all.[6]

Wheat and grapes. Cross and crown. Life out of death. But the gospel enacted in martyrdom needs to be told in greater detail. Karl Olsson describes the event as follows:

> Three Covenant missionaries: Dr. Alik Berg, Esther Nordlund, and Martha Anderson, were on their way to a conference at Kingchow in the southern part of the field when they were shot by bandits. The circumstances are significant. The three missionaries boarded a truck in Siangyang on January 7, 1948. There had been some trouble with bandits and six or eight soldiers were hired to guard the truck. About sixty miles south of Siangyang the road snakes through deserted hills. Here fifty bandits, scaring off the hired guard, stopped the truck and ordered the occupants out. Then they proceeded to rob them. When they discovered that Dr. Berg was a foreigner, they took his passport. The robbers then picked up their loot and began moving.

Normally this would have been the end of the incident. But for unknown reasons, four of them returned, singled out Berg, and asked if he and the women were American citizens. Berg did not answer. Then with the words, "Americans are the worst of all; they have done China much harm," the bandit leader shot Berg through the head. At the sound of the shot Martha Anderson began to sob, and the bandit, assuming that she was a relative of Berg, killed her also. By this time some of the Chinese passengers were pleading that the killing would stop, but the bandits were not satisfied. When they turned to Esther Nordlund, she is reported to have said, "Yes, you may kill me too." Thereupon she also was shot.[7]

When the news of Martha's death was received at Covenant headquarters in Chicago, Rev. Clarence A. Nelson, her former pastor and at that time president of Minnehaha Academy, was asked to take the news to the Anderson family. It is reported that when Rev. Adolph Anderson heard of the death of his daughter, he spoke out of a stunned silence, saying, "What great honor has been bestowed on us as a family that our daughter should be a martyr for Christ! The Lord has given and the Lord has taken away. Blessed be the name of the Lord."[8]

"Not in defeat but in triumph Martha sealed her vow with her life. In that same sense of quiet triumph, Salem has given its beautiful gift to missions."[9] But Martha's martyrdom has also been her gift to Salem, in putting into a faith confessed and a life lived the passion of a martyr strain that cannot be forgotten as long as the story is told. A woman's shattered alabaster jar!

Covenant Women

During the middle and late 1960s there was a strong trend nationally to unify women's work in Covenant churches. After two years of careful study, and looking toward the move into a new community, Salem women voted to disband the Martha Society and Chen King U Society, joining together as Covenant Women. A single organization with smaller groups for study and fellowship appeared to be a more effective way to proceed. Because of strong loyalties to both organizations, the decision to unite was not made without considerable emotional struggle. However, on September 9, 1969, at a moving service of Holy Communion, the change was consummated. Dorothy Anderson, a member of Chen King U, became the first president of Covenant Women.

With new challenges to face in walking untried paths in women's ministry, the influence of Salem on the national body is significant. The spirit of *Mor i Vall* was again present in two of Salem's women:

- Anna (Mrs. Eng) Olson (1896-1953). Following her death in March of 1953, a service of dedication was held on October 23. That day a tree was planted on the campus of Minnehaha Academy, with a stone and bronze plaque in her memory. President Arthur W. Anderson characterized Mrs. Eng Olson as "a leader who caught the pulse-beat of every community of which she was a part" and, by her active commitment to the full scope of denominational and conference work, was "the ideal of what the total Covenant can become." In the 1940s she was chair of the Covenant Women Christian Morals Civics Committee, and in the local scene she put her ideals to work in the temperance cause. Her lips did not speak blandly of "crooked politics"; she attended rallies, took part in efforts to remove bad leaders and replace them with good, and once ran for the office of state representative. But, like *Mor i Vall*, she remained always the Pietist who also caught the pulse-beat of the gospel. George Bergquist recalls from his youth, one Sunday evening, attending an evangelistic meeting at Salem: "I was sitting next to Mrs. Eng Olson, whose husband owned a large produce firm in the Minneapolis Central Market. At the end of the meeting, the preacher gave the traditional invitation to those who might want to come forward as a symbol of their dedication to the Lord. I hesitated, and then Mrs. Olson gently whispered the same invitation in my ear. I rose and walked forward. That was a central milepost in my life, and I remain thankful to Mrs. Olson to this day."
- Erma Chinander (1914-) began work at Salem in 1937 as church secretary and parish worker. In 1944 she went to North Park to continue her education, and later to Augsburg College in Minneapolis to prepare for a teaching career. She taught Bible at Minnehaha Acad-

emy and in 1953 became administrative assistant to her former pastor, Rev. Clarence A. Nelson, president of North Park. She continued in a similar position when he became president of the Covenant. During these years in Chicago Erma was active in Covenant Women, and in 1969 she was elected national president, a position leading to the office of secretary of Covenant Women in 1972. She was the first woman to serve on the Council of Administrators of the Evangelical Covenant Church. In 1980 she retired and eventually moved back to Minneapolis and to Salem. With her sister, Vivian, she now resides at Covenant Manor in Golden Valley.

Sister Servants

While the early minutes of the congregation refer to a group of women designated as deaconesses who were already active before the formal organization took place in 1888, women did not hold church office until much later. The traditional office of deaconess was recognized by the call-

ing of Alma Johnson (1879-1946) in 1913 to visit and care for the sick and poor.[10] But it was not until April 1, 1922, that the deacons submitted a proposal to the congregation that deaconesses be appointed to assist them in the task of caretaking. With approval by the church board, the deacons were asked to submit the names of women who they believed could best serve. Instead of calling them deaconesses, however, the deacons recommended that they be called Sister Servants of the Church. Whether this term elevated their position or side-stepped the issue of assigning them full status as deacons is unclear. In any case, eight names were proposed and accepted.

The record of Sister Servants would not be complete without mention of the long and distinguished service of Olga (Green) Gustafson (1896-1968). Following in the steps of Alma Johnson, Erma Chinander, Dorothy

Lundstrom (Balch), and Lorraine Bjorklund (Pratt), Olga was the last to be called a parish worker or church missionary, a position in which she served for almost twenty years (1948-1967). Though her churchly duties were many—serving as secretary to the pastor, turning out the weekly Sunday bulletins, sending frequent church mailings, teaching and working with all age groups from children to older people—she will perhaps best be remembered for her countless visits to homes in Northeast, where she ministered to both the physical and the spiritual needs of countless numbers of people. She was a true caretaker!

The long procession of women in Salem's story, including those named above and many others not named who served in a multitude of ways, prepared the way for future women in ministry. One can only wonder what "dear Greta" or Kajsa or the other sisters in the Olsson home on Monroe Street might think of the changes in women's roles at Salem a hundred years later:

- Women not only preparing but serving Holy Communion
- Frances Decker as the first ordained woman on the pastoral staff
- Judy Edlund as the first woman chairperson of the congregation, offering her skills of leadership during a critical time of transition.

With the changing role of women in society and its impact on the church, it is not surprising that toward the century's end one would hear a few voices expressing anxiety that men in the church might respond by saying, "Let the women do it!" A more positive reading, however, would see in the changes a new partnership emerging between women and men, with the result of shaping a congregation's identity and empowering leadership in fresh new ways of ministry. *Mor i Vall* might look down from some higher balcony and say, "*Ja*, that's good!"

LOVE
GOOD NEWS FOR CHILDREN

8

Telling the Next Generation, Part I

While early Mission Friends held a view of the church as consisting of only believing Christians, they also wanted to make sure that children had place in the congregation. For this reason they continued to baptize children and confirm young people—not with a Lutheran understanding that these were rites of admission into full membership in the church, but as "preparatory and promissory rites which incorporate the child into the Christian community, proclaim the interest of the church in [the child] and which witness constantly to the necessity of a full commitment to Christ."[1] By the act of baptism Mission Friends sought to make clear in a beautiful and celebrative way that children have place due to their own intrinsic nature and worth, and that they come to baptism as those already in the kingdom. In the words of the 1964 Covenant book of worship, "They belong with all who believe to the body of Christ, through the covenant made in him."[2]

Later on when there were parents who chose in a similar, celebrative way to present their children for an act of blessing, it was not with the notion that children have value only as adult believers, but that the responsibility for telling the next generation lays on parents and congregation a sacred urgency. In either case, Mission Friends saw the importance of an act of conversion or at least decision when a child reached the age of accountability. Such a living experience of grace lay behind the telling.

A Serious Intentionality

A community concerned to include the next generation in its faith and passion worries a great deal about getting the biblical story safely entrusted to its young. The early minutes from the mission house on Jefferson Street express such a recurring anxiety and care. While one assumes some form of instructing the young from the beginning, the first reference to an organized effort occurs in the minutes of January 1, 1890, reporting the election of Sunday school officers, with L.M. Lindquist as superintendent.[3]

Seven years later the first annual report from the Sunday school appears in the church minutes, recording an enrollment of 268 children with 230 in attendance every Sunday! The teaching staff and officers were 32 with 30 present every Sunday, giving an average attendance for the year

of 277! By the turn of the century there were 350 children enrolled, indicating a mission house bulging with children.

For a number of years the Sunday school was held following the preaching service from 12:15 to 1:30 in the afternoon and was divided into two sections, one for small children unable to read and the other for older children. There were as many as thirty classes, including one for young men and another for young women. The adults also had a Bible class.

Despite the lack of space, graded lessons, and other teaching resources we take for granted today, the purpose was clear and unambiguous:

> The Sunday School has as its goal to win children's hearts for Jesus, and this work has been carried on as before. Flower cards with Bible verses have been distributed to the children each Sunday. A special award card has been given to those children who have brought friends or playmates to Sunday school. I pray that our Almighty God will richly bless the Sunday school in its work during the upcoming year of 1897.[4]

Cherished Memories

When the congregation moved to Central Avenue, the Sunday school experienced remarkable growth but retained its patterns of organization. Classes were segregated by sex and met in all parts of the building. When a child could read Swedish, she would be promoted from the Sunday school in the basement to the Sunday school in the sanctuary. And in the sanctuary classes were held on the main floor and in the balcony. "Upstairs, Downstairs," the memories of people and place are many:

- In earlier days at Salem the "Golden Text" in Swedish was always lettered out each Sunday by alphabet cards on a blackboard suspended from the ceiling in front of the Sunday school.
- Children were taught the polite practice of calling the venerable men of our church "uncle." Thus, we spoke in Swedish of Farbro Lundquist, who was Sunday school superintendent of the primary department for many years, and Farbro Larson and Farbro Lindquist.[5]
- One Sunday my brother and I told our parents that we needed to get to Sunday school especially early, and when we got there we had a great time in the empty sanctuary, sailing paper airplanes from the heights of the balcony down to the main floor. I don't recall the "Golden Text" that we memorized for that Sunday, nor do I remember whether we recovered all the airplanes we had launched. But I well recall the dedication, patience, and loving kindness of the teachers who made Sunday school at Salem a growing experience for my

brother and me, and for our friends.[6]

Newer Strategies

With the gradual shift to English in the late 1920s, the door was opened for more effective ways of Sunday school teaching. Even though it was a modest concession to change, Sunday school texts were now available in both Swedish and English. Nathaniel Franklin, who was elected to the office of Sunday school secretary for the Covenant in 1919, introduced a graded lesson system that was suited to the needs of different ages.[7] Before this, the same curriculum was offered to everyone, with the assumption that people became Christians in the same way. With a graded system there was a recognition that telling the gospel story meant addressing the needs of each age differently.

The newer strategies of Christian education also acknowledged that Sunday school was a better way of doing evangelism than more militant forms. One of the outstanding achievements of Rev. Clarence Nelson's ministry was his introduction of a teacher training class in the Sunday school, most likely the first among Covenant churches. Older members who were enrolled in the three classes graduated by him recall with appreciation the help and inspiration they received. The results of this newer strategy show in the growth of Sunday school enrollment. Despite the space factor on Central Avenue, the size of the Sunday school as reported in the annual report of 1938 was 725, including the cradle roll, teachers, and officers.

Mother Tongue

If there was a serious intentionality in passing on the faith to the next generation through the Sunday school, *how* that faith would safely be entrusted to the young was a continuing source of anxiety and concern. Discussions of finding the means and personnel for preserving the mother tongue occupy as prominent a place in early congregational meetings as taking care of the poor. Pastor C.V. Bowman gave voice to this concern in his pastoral report of January 2, 1905:

In our activities, it is coming more and more to the point where we need to make special effort to interest the young people growing up. Children among us, although born of Swedish parents, are not familiar enough with the mother tongue. It is a problem difficult to solve—how we shall handle that, what we must do, or what it would take to reach their hearts and win their interest. While we wait for a fortunate solution to that question we should show these young people friendship, love and confidence as long as possible.[8]

The "Swede School"

As early as July 7, 1890, Pastor K.A. Jonson reported to the congregation that, with support from parents, a Swedish weekday school had begun on June 23; the teacher was to receive thirty dollars a month. Each year a decision was made to continue this summer school and to obtain teachers. The school ran for eight weeks each summer, and a fee was charged each student. Though it was intended to be self-supporting, the school usually ran a small deficit each year. And finding qualified teachers each summer was a continuing struggle.

The instruction consisted of reading, spelling, writing, and an attempt at composition—with the intent, of course, of teaching the Swedish language. Each class would begin with prayer and Bible reading, together with some remarks about the reading. Among the several teachers who

came from North Park, one teacher appears to have provided a more systematic study of the Bible itself.

> Lesson time was from 9 till 12 in the morning and from 1:30 to 3:30 in the afternoon when we focused on reading from the Bible. . . . What I have always strived for was not only that the children learn to speak, write and read Swedish but to imprint on their hearts reverence for God and his word and abhorrence of sin in hope that at least some seed falls in good soil.

Though attendance in the early 1900s reached as high as 152 students, one detects a gradual decline in both interest and attendance. The teacher quoted above makes this revealing comment in his report to the congregation: "Fifty children have attended school of which 22 have been present for the entire time. Of the others, 19 were present the first month and 9 the other. Only one pupil, Ingeborg Klarstrom, was present every day."[9]

The Language Question

With today's understanding and commitment to the church as an inclusive community, the casual observer might find it difficult to appreciate Salem's struggle and pain over the language question. Three observations may help. First, Salem's struggle was not unlike the experience of other ethnic groups. In this ethnic congregation, Swedish was the language of worship. Preaching and hearing the gospel in one's native tongue, singing the hymns and saying the prayers, were the cherished means of grace forming the members' primal experience of Christ. It was similar to hearing missionaries on furlough exclaim after a service of worship in English that it was "like a soft, warm spring shower upon a thirsty field."

Furthermore, their purpose was not to make Swedes out of non-Swedes, but to bring souls "out of darkness into the marvelous light." And given the floodtide of Swedish immigration both preceding and following the turn of the century, the field among their fellow countrymen was ripe for harvest. The new arrivals needed to hear the old, old story in their mother tongue.

One further compelling reason for preserving the Swedish language was the fear of assimilation into the surrounding culture. One looks back with not a little humor on the intense discussions involving requests that "magic lantern shows" be shown in the sanctuary. However, as a symbol of Americanization, with its "mushrooming entertainment industry fostering the movie stars—the culture of liberated sexuality, bootleg hooch, and sordid private living; the parallel explosion of the athletic world and the expansion and popularization of the radio and gramophone . . . as entertainment media,"[10] the fear is understandable. They were resident aliens, a people set apart, living "in the world" but not "of the world." They were a people of the Spirit, unashamed of being misfits—if not a bit odd—for the sake of their identity as the twice-born.

A transition to English began in the late 1920s under the ministry of Rev. Clarence Nelson, who was fluent in both languages. Through wise and patient leadership, he was able to make the transition less painful for the older generation while lending encouragement and support to the younger. The first step in the transition was the use of English at Sunday evening services and at church business meetings; then on alternating Sundays, Swedish and English. Finally on September 6, 1938, the congregation voted that all English be used at the Sunday morning services beginning on October 1, thus signaling the completion of the transition. However, Swedish services continued to be conducted in the lower auditorium for several years, and occasionally for festivals, such as church anniversaries.

Americanization

When the clouds of a devastating World War I darkened the skies, the cost of being different would be high, making the language question itself a heavy cross to bear. Other ethnic groups, especially Germans, experienced similar difficulties. Winds of change were blowing, and painful decisions would lie ahead for an ethnic community. Speaking of the impact of World War I on the congregation, Eric Dahlhielm, an earlier historian of Salem's story, tells of the pain:

> The young men of the church were taken away to training camps or to France. Epidemics of influenza swept over the country. Day after day the minister went from sickbed to funeral, from funeral to

> sick bed. The right to worship in the language of our fathers was threatened and, in some instances, very much circumscribed. The government made strong efforts to use the church as an agency for raising money and spreading war propaganda. The followers of Christ were asked to hate, and to their everlasting shame, many of them hearkened unto men more than unto God. Indeed, those were days that tried a man's soul.[11]

World War II would complete the process of Salem becoming an American church, yet still struggling with its identity as a people set apart. The Swede school would be only a distant memory for an older generation—and not the most pleasant memory, at that! In its place would be a summer daily vacation Bible school—not for eight weeks, but for two, and in more recent years one week. The curricula would contain biblical themes that would awaken the interests and needs of children in more engaging ways.[12]

"Let the Children Come..."

Whenever the invitation of Jesus is given and heard and there is not room enough for all who come, that is a hopeful sign to a people anxious to tell the gospel story to the next generation. Whether in mission house, tabernacle, or church, the serious intentionality in the telling led sooner or later to an enlargement or renovation of facilities.

In the fall of 1890 the congregation decided to add a school room twenty-six by thirty-two feet on the north side of the mission house on Jefferson Street. Its completion became the occasion for painting the exterior of the whole building the following spring, using a light color—one pound of yellow ochre to each ten pounds of white lead. They also laid a sidewalk on 17th Avenue six feet wide and 132 feet long, at a cost of seventy-nine dollars; Mr. Westlind, in turn, donated twenty-five dollars to the church treasury. That year also saw Mr. L. Johnson filling in the adjoining lots and erecting a fence around the church property.

On Central Avenue, space for expanding children's and youth ministry was a continuing problem, as indicated above. In the fall of 1946 the house south of the church facing Central Avenue, where Alma Johnson

had lived for many years, was purchased and used for Sunday school classes. Two years later it was torn down to be replaced by two buildings of a more temporary character, each twenty-four by forty feet, located on the rear of the lot. The first building was replaced by a Christian education building in 1954, providing further space for offices, Sunday school rooms, and a new heating plant.

Less than ten years following the move to New Brighton, the need for more space led to a further building program named Phase Two. This included more space for Sunday school classes and youth ministry, a social hall-gymnasium, a kitchen, further space for church offices, and an elevator for the handicapped. The new building was dedicated in memory of Pastor Paul E. Stohlberg, who died before seeing its completion. The litany of dedication was read at a dinner in the new social hall on November 17, 1979, with Rev. Craig W. Nelson, president of Minnehaha Academy, as guest speaker.[13]

A Ministry of Hospitality

While providing physical space for children and youth has been a high priority in Salem's story, another kind of space including hospitality to the young has been an underlying theme. In Pastor C.V. Bowman's pastoral report reflecting concern for the young, he concluded by getting down to specifics:

> Seek even to greet the strangers who come to church and the young who go among us . . . we ought, in fact, give them a songbook to sing from at our meeting. There probably is not a congregation or church found in our city that is so badly off as song books are concerned. And we must get that remedied before we lose too much. It is sad to see from the platform strangers and young people in large numbers on Sunday night and probably not one in 50 persons has a song book to sing from. Let us seek to have that remedied before the annual meeting ends today. Let us make every effort at our meeting to come closer to the young and to visiting strangers. But above all, let us pray that God may carry out his work with them.[14]

Before the meeting ended, the congregation voted to purchase six hundred copies of a song book called *Sions Glädjebud* (Zion's Glad Message), four hundred copies with music and two hundred containing words only. Telling the next generation was that practical and urgent!

NOVEM
FRUIT

9

Telling the Next Generation, Part II

If the first generation worried about getting the biblical story safely entrusted to its offspring, it must have been reassured to know that these were trustworthy children who would responsibly receive and preserve the inheritance. Of course, as every parent knows, the outcome of faith in the next generation is never an exact replica of that of the forebears. That is a mystery between the generations which cannot be penetrated or controlled. Still, the gospel story would be told and the earlier mystique of the Mission Friends would survive.

Trustworthy Children

On December 30, 1891, seven young men in the congregation met to determine how best to carry on work among the youth. Following the reading of 1 Peter 4, they elected officers: Simon O. Lindahl, president; P. Larson, vice-president; F. Lindquist, treasurer; and C.R. Martinson, secretary. Concluding that the young women could help, the seven men invited them to a joint meeting in January. Thereafter it became an active society, with the young women forming a sewing group and the young men serving as ushers in the church. Together they raised funds for mission work, visited the sick and poor, met for prayer on Sunday mornings, and held a service of praise and fellowship on Sunday afternoons. By the end of the first year the group numbered thirty-two young people. And at the annual meeting of the congregation on January 1, 1898, a motion was made inviting the Young People's Society to affiliate with the church.

The story of Simon O. Lindahl needs telling. President of the society for sixteen years, he was also supported by the group in a railroad ministry called the Immigrant Mission. His task was to meet incoming trains at railroad depots in Minneapolis, where he no doubt became friend and brother to many a lonesome, perhaps penniless and homeless, newcomer seeking a better life in the New World. When Lindahl died in 1908, the church and the Young People's Society shared the expenses for his funeral. There was apparently no surviving family member except a nephew in his native Norway.

A further glimpse into the life of young people in the immigrant community of Salem is given in a letter written to relatives in Sweden by a young girl who was a member of the society.

> Yes, now both Christmas and New Year's have passed. We went to Julotta on Christmas morning. In the evening we had our children's festival. On New Year's Day papa was in church the whole day. They had their annual meeting. The picture I am sending is of our church and pastor. We have had the pastor since last summer. He is the best Swedish speaker in America. Ethel goes to read for him this year and shall continue next year. She will then be confirmed and finish school at the same time. New Year's Eve the young people in our church had a sleigh ride. We rode 14 miles out to Turtle Lake where

one of our boys has their summer place. The boy's mama went out there the day before so it would be warm when we came. We left Minneapolis at 7:00 p.m. and arrived there at 12:00 p.m. After we had oyster stew and candy and nuts. At 4:00 a.m. we left and got to Minneapolis at 7:00 a.m. Oh, how tired we were! We slept almost all New Year's Day. . . . We have had meetings at church lasting three weeks and in February we will be having a revival meeting. I have joined the Young People's Society now. We have our meetings at 5:00 p.m. every Sunday night. Pastor Kling is our chairman. . . .[1]

Religious Earnestness

The objectives of the Young People's Society remained simple and undeviating, as the minutes book of 1938-1962 makes clear: "to win other young people for Christ and edify those who are Christians." How they managed to meet those objectives was more complex. In the late 1930s, with a membership of over one hundred, their earnestness shows in the following committee structure:

Program	Decoration
Social	Publicity
Membership	Sunshine
Refreshment	Fellowship
Relief	Dishwashing

Through the reports that each committee gave at quarterly business meetings, one observes the high degree of accountability in the group.

Experience in both organization and planning provided a remarkably rich training ground for church leadership that would continue into the years of Salem's burgeoning growth in New Brighton. In the printed programs of the society from 1928 to 1938, religious earnestness shows in the diversity of themes, topics, speakers, leaders, and musical talent. The winter program of 1933 featured a study of the Letter to the Hebrews under the theme "The Better Life," with subtopics such as "Moses and the Better Leader," "Aaron and the Better High Priest," "Tabernacle and the Better Covenant," and "Sacrifice and the Better Sacrifice." Hardly trivial topics!

During his ministry Pastor Clarence Nelson was a frequent speaker at the Sunday afternoon meetings on subjects such as baptism, the Lord's Supper, and the Atonement. Debates would be held on such current issues as whether Christians should participate in war. Predictive of their

future roles in theological education, both Donald Frisk[2] and Paul L. Holmer[3] were speakers on topics they would later pass on to several generations of theological students—the latter speaking in 1936 on "Jesus as a Man of Prayer" and in 1938 on "The Idea of God."

Reaching Out

But earnestness was expressed in other ways. While there was an eagerness to explore the biblical and theological themes close to their spiritual roots, they were just as eager to test and broaden their learnings by listening to those outside their own community—to explore ideas from guest speakers over a broad spectrum ranging from David Swenson of the University of Minnesota to Sverre Norborg of Augsburg College; to enter the cultural world of art and music (much to the discomfort of some of their elders); and, not least of all, to explore relationships with other churches and people of diverse backgrounds.

Such reaching out was in part due to the Americanization of the younger generation, both in reacting to a closed society and in accommodating to the contemporary world. After all, they were Americans. Living and working in the world, going to college and university, and (for many) serving in the armed forces, they needed to know that the Christian faith could not only survive but flourish in the culture and society beyond the walls of the Tabernacle at 18½ and Central avenues!

It was by such earnestness and passion to learn and explore that the story and tradition of immigrant forebears would live on and be passed to the next generation and beyond. Even when the Young People's Society would yield to other forms of youth ministry with widely different accents, themes, and constituencies (which was true especially in New Brighton), the inheritance would remain intact.

"Crisis" Evangelism

As the story of Salem's beginnings makes clear, a personal encounter with the crucified and risen Jesus—however that encounter might be described—has been the centerpiece of belonging. At times the persuasion toward such a meeting with Christ was too aggressive and manipulative, but it has always remained a central concern in telling the next generation. It would be difficult to count how many of Salem's young people have been touched and dedicated to Christ because of Bible camp. As one tired little boy was overheard saying to his father as he got off the bus after a week at camp, "Dad, do I have to wait a whole year to go back?"

The first mention of Bible camp is found in the young people's minutes book, September 30, 1938, where one of its members gave what is described as "an interesting report of the Lake Koronis Conference which was a week of unforgettable blessings for our 41 Salem campers."[4] That camp, where the Northwest Conference began holding summer meetings in the early 1930s, was open to both families and young people throughout the state. It was well attended, with gifted speakers and musicians from the Covenant. Early in 1939 the Young People's Society sponsored an essay contest on "The Value of Attending Lake Koronis Bible Camp," providing two yearly scholarships to a boy and a girl for a free week at camp.

In 1942 when the camp at Lake Koronis was no longer open to teenagers, the Twin City Youth Organization sponsored a Hi-League camp at Matawah. Later in the 1940s, under the leadership of Pastor Clarence Agard and Olga Gustafson, Bible camps were held at Park Point, Hinckley, and Matawah, with many Salem young people involved as camp counselors.

Covenant Pines

With transitions in camping space and changes in constituency, a deeply felt need in both conference and local congregations led in the early 1950s to the forming of a Twin Cities Bible Camp Committee consisting of pastors, Hi-League counselors, and representatives of church boards. The task of finding suitable property and reporting their findings was given to one of Salem's members, Curtis W. Johnson, and two other Covenant laymen from Twin Cities churches.

The story is told that at a dinner party of Salem members, Curtis Johnson, who was the first chairman of the newly formed committee, shared the need for such a camp and told the guests he had found an ideal piece of property known as Frontier Camp at McGregor, Minnesota. Because prompt action was needed to hold the property, the group contributed enough money that evening for a down payment on what is now Covenant Pines Bible Camp.

As with many other Covenant churches in the Twin Cities, a "lovework" relationship began between Salem and the camp that continues to shape the spiritual life of all ages. Many lay persons have spent countless Saturdays and weekends upgrading the physical facilities of the camp. Covenant Pines is now also a winter facility, employing a full-time staff. At Salem the Warren Green Memorial Scholarship Fund was established in 1952 by Lawrence and Mildred Green for honor students in confirmation. This scholarship was given in memory of their son, Warren, who died in the service of his country in November of 1951, and it continued until 1972.

While the camping program has had a high priority at Salem in telling the next generation, the Covenant High Congress begun by the denomination's Board of Christian Education has also had considerable impact on its youth. CHIC, as it is known, is a one-time event for every high schooler in the Covenant, held every three years in various locations in the country. Preceding this triennial event, young people and their parents together with the congregation have become involved in fund-raising programs in order to help make this event available to as many young people as wish to attend. Many lasting and telling moments in meeting Christ have occurred in these national gatherings—one of the happier sides to the institutionalizing of a revival movement.

"Saturation" Evangelism

The first and only reference to confirmation in the minutes of congregational meetings between 1888 and 1901 occurs on December 7, 1891. So significant is it both to Covenant history and to Salem's story that the entry must be reported: "Since Professor David Nyvall wished to come to our mission house to hold confirmation classes for our young people, it was decided to greet and welcome him and to utilize Tuesday evenings for this."[5]

The role of confirmation in the upheavals of the Reformation needs comment. Luther retained both the instruction and the rite of confirmation but reoriented it toward a young person's admission to the Lord's Supper. The word *catechism* means primarily oral instruction through questions and answers, to be conducted in home, church, and school. Those

"ABCs" constituting the minimal knowledge required for a Christian were the Ten Commandments, Apostles' Creed, Lord's Prayer, and the texts of the institution of baptism and the Lord's Supper. These "profound simplicities" were the throbbing heart of Luther's emphasis in the *Small and Large Catechisms*: that young people might know the One in whom they are to believe, and in knowing him might participate with joy in the Sunday liturgy of word and sacrament.[6]

Among early Mission Friends, confirmation was retained as a further means of telling the next generation and acting on one's baptism. The earliest confirmation texts used in Covenant churches were based on Luther's *Small Catechism*, but with accents clearly reflecting the concerns of Pietism. Taught by the earliest version of *Kristlig Troslära* (later translated into English in a small blue book, "The Christian Faith"), and continued in the texts that followed, generations of Covenanters would know by heart such catechetical teaching as "What is the highest and most important knowledge? The highest and most important knowledge is to know God and his son Jesus Christ (John 17:3)." Or "What is sin? Sin is all that in thought, word and deed is contrary to the will of God, whether it be a transgression of what God has forbidden or an omission of what he has commanded (1 John 3:4)."

Whereas Lutheran confirmation had as its primary purpose the admission of a young person to Holy Communion, Covenant confirmation sought by both biblical instruction and pastoral conversation to precipitate a crisis of conversion as the means of access to the fellowship of believers. George Bergquist's recollection of confirmation in the 1930s might evoke the memories of many:

> In the one-year confirmation class which met every Saturday morning, the routine that stands out most clearly in my mind was memorizing the catechism. On Confirmation Sunday the class occupied the choir loft up there behind the pulpit, and at one point the minister randomly asked individual confirmands one question or another. We were expected to respond promptly and correctly, and I recall that all of us responded perfectly that Sunday morning.[7]

Delivering a farewell address on behalf of the class of 1931, Bergquist had said:

> The hours we have spent together during the last eight months, although brief, have been of great value to us. We have really enjoyed coming together and studying about the nobler things in life. We have recently completed a systemized study of the Bible and its teaching. The class has had opportunities to decide for Christ, which a number of the members have done. The friendships that have been formed here will influence us greatly in our life's journey. And thinking of the future, we wish to tell you we are not going away from Christ and the Church. Many of us have already entered into the work of the Junior League. We are determined to continue in the Sunday school and later become reliable Christian members of this church.[8]

Enter David Nyvall

In the statement quoted above that "Professor David Nyvall wished to come to our mission house to hold confirmation classes for our young people," we uncover a remarkable story both in Salem's history and in the Covenant's. As Karl Olsson says, "No one played a more significant role in the shaping of the Covenant than David Nyvall."[9]

Shortly after his arrival in America, this bright young graduate of

Uppsala University, grandson of *Mor i Vall*, who was planning on a career in medicine, met Pastor E. August Skogsbergh at the second Annual Meeting of the Covenant held in Rockford, Illinois, in September of 1886. This meeting marked a turning point in the young immigrant's life. Evidently impressed by the opening sermon of the Annual Meeting, which Nyvall had been invited to deliver, Skogsbergh offered him a teaching position in his newly established school in Minneapolis, then located at Riverside and 25th Avenue. Accepting his offer, Nyvall entered classroom teaching for the first time. He also met his future wife, Lovisa Gustava Skogsbergh, sister of the pastor, whom he married one year later on December 29, 1887.

After a brief pastorate in Sioux City, Iowa, the Covenant called Nyvall to serve as an assistant to Professor Fridolf Risberg in the Swedish department at the Chicago Theological Seminary. In September of 1890, following the Covenant Annual Meeting in Galesburg, Illinois, he returned to Minneapolis to teach again at "Skogsbergh's school," which was now located in the Swedish Tabernacle.

During the time Professor Nyvall was holding confirmation classes on Jefferson Street along with his other teaching responsibilities, he was also

deeply engaged in formulating ideas and plans for a Covenant school which would be not only a Bible school but an institution providing the Covenant with a solid educational base for both lay people and clergy. In 1891 Skogsbergh's school became, by denominational decision, the Covenant school, to which David Nyvall was appointed president in the following spring. This eventually led to the controversial decision to move the school from Minneapolis to Chicago. There in 1894 it became a name and institution, the Swedish Evangelical Mission Covenant College (now North Park College and Theological Seminary), as well as a building, Old Main, which was dedicated on June 14, 1894.

Meanwhile, for at least two years the Jefferson Street mission house was standing knee-deep in the stream of history-making, most likely not knowing either the importance of who was teaching the young people or to what extent David Nyvall would influence countless other young people for generations to come.

Strong Role Models

Telling the next generation requires more than good teachers, whether in confirmation, Sunday school, or pulpit; it must have strong role models. While there is a growing literature today about the diminishing role of men in the home, workplace, and voluntary associations, Salem's story from the beginning to the present is a story of strong male leadership.

During the years 1938 to 1958 the minutes of Salem's Brotherhood record an inspiring commitment to being and doing church—not only by the planning of inspirational programs, decorating the church for Christmas, purchasing a lighted cross on Central Avenue with the words "Salem" and "Welcome," contributing to the construction of Burgh Hall on the campus of North Park, giving to a Covenant pension fund for retired pastors, and serving the yearly smörgåsbord—but also by building bridges between the generations through active support of Boy Scouts, the Twin Cities Basketball League, the yearly Fathers' and Sons' Banquet, and maintaining contact with the young men from Salem serving in the armed forces in World War II. When the national organization Covenant Men of America came into being on June 18, 1963, Harlan Erickson, one of Salem's active laymen, was elected president. He served for three years until his sudden death on May 20, 1966.

Nurturing Evangelism

When Salem moved to New Brighton, the congregation wanted to find new ways of getting in touch with the surrounding community. Rev. K. Wesley Olson, then assistant pastor, approached Pamela Carlson with the idea of starting a nursery school at Salem. At the time there were few nursery schools in the area and little supervision by the state Department of Human Services or Department of Education. The motivating factor for Salem was to provide a practical service to the new neighborhood, with the possibility of making contact with young families of preschool children in the area. With few local or state regulations, it was easy to start such a school.

The first class of twenty students began in the fall of 1971, with Ruth Hultgren, wife of Dayton D. Hultgren (president of United Theological Seminary), as head teacher. The program was held in one of the lower level classrooms of the new building. Five hundred dollars was budgeted to purchase a few toys, some records, glue, paper, scissors, and other necessities; and the tuition paid by the students was to cover the cost of teachers' salaries. The school has supported itself ever since.[10]

From its humble beginnings, the preschool grew rapidly. Pam Carlson has continued to direct the school, reporting on a regular basis to the Children's Commission (earlier the Board of Christian Education). As evidence of the good reputation of the preschool in New Brighton, it is no longer a surprise—but still very exciting—to find the church halls lined with parents who come early on the morning of registration, anxious to see their children enrolled in the school.

As an outreach ministry of the church, the school from its beginning has been concerned about how best to tell the gospel story in a context of nurturing love. Their approach is a simple one: "If God's love can shine through the teachers, helping them care for the children and their families in a nurturing way, regardless of their religious, ethnic or social background, then Christ will do his part to bring the families into our church.[11]

Over the years the Salem preschool has had children from a variety of religious backgrounds and many countries, including China, Korea, Ethiopia, Iceland, and India. Furthermore, the school has accepted children with various physical handicaps, learning disabilities, and behavioral problems. Currently the Mounds View School District places several of its "special needs students" in the preschool each year.

From its beginnings to the present, the Salem preschool has grown to a school with six classes, touching the lives of 120 children and their families each week. Without any sense of aggressive evangelism, yet with a commitment to loving, nurturing relationships with children, it has been one of Salem's most effective means of evangelical witness. Many nursery school families have been drawn into the School of Christian Living, daily vacation Bible school, and Mothers' Fellowship. Many have joined Salem, becoming active, contributing members of the congregation.

A Matter of Fidelity

Behind our predecessors' serious intent of telling the biblical story to the next generation, there was a recognition—sometimes with hesitation and even reluctance—that it could never be done only once or by a single method or experience, or even only in one's own mother tongue. Likewise, it was a matter of utmost urgency that there be new participants in telling the story, so that in moving to new times and places each new retelling would be an event of saving, transforming significance.

What moves one in Salem's story is the undeviating fidelity of earlier generations in telling the old, old story. And with it, there was always the continuing struggle to find better ways of telling it and so reenter the primal event of the story again, each time with "more discernment and awed mystery."[12] If the gospel remains a compelling passion among those telling it now in ways that impact every aspect of contemporary life, both personal and communal, the next generation will catch on!

Postscript

An Unfinished Story

In telling Salem's story, one feels the frustration of the biblical author who comes to the end of a roll call of the faithful by throwing up his hands in despair: "And what more should I say? For time would fail me to tell of . . . ," followed by a continuing recital of the unnamed heroes of faith (Hebrews 11:32).

So with the story of Salem. There is always more that could be said. Perhaps from some longer view what has been left unsaid may be more significant. For example, the early church minutes from the 1890s record discussions of a mission outpost in Columbia Heights—a discussion that bore fruit years later in the building of a chapel which, while no longer in existence, touched many lives for Christ.

Another story could be told of lengthy discussions in the late 1980s which led to the decision to parent a new congregation in Shoreview. As a result, the mother church, now on "this side of the river," set apart Rev. James L. Anderson, one of Salem's associate pastors for eight years, as founding pastor, and gave members as well as financial support toward the formation of a congregation in the fall of 1991.

A Story of Risk-Taking

Being a mission church always involves a certain amount of risk-taking. One could tell of other ministries on Central Avenue born out of passion and concern, such as:

- a radio broadcast
- drive-in theater services
- tent meetings
- street meetings
- a program of hospitality to neighborhood families

There have also been ministries in New Brighton that have been imaginative and innovative, including:

- musical groups such as Peace in Light under the direction of Ron White
- a church band led by Betty Krause
- drama productions produced by Barbara Lord Collings
- the Swedish Singers led by Marillyn Goolsbee
- a signing ministry for the hearing-handicapped by Karen Scheibe
- a bell choir begun by teenagers directed by Reda Johnson
- a sister-church relationship with Community Covenant
- Sunday evening healing services
- significant youth ministries of social outreach led by Greg Fondell

Like the Columbia Heights chapel, some of these ventures in mission failed. Others met a temporary need and then passed into oblivion. Still others continue to serve the mission effectively, such as the decision in the 1980s to move from a three board structure of leadership to the church council system. But whether success or failure, each made its contribution to the ongoing story of Salem, even as each bore fruit in its season. Such risk-taking for the sake of Christ gives continuing meaning to the name we were first given, *Mission Friends*, and to the first name of the Covenant, *Missionsförbundet,* a bonding together for mission.

A Sober Reminder

From a revival movement over a hundred years ago to the institution which Salem has become today, there is need for a larger perspective of history in telling the story. The original character of a movement such as ours is inevitably modified in time by the natural processes of birth and death, of growth and maturity. H. Richard Niebuhr provides a helpful observation:

> By its very nature the sectarian type of organization is valid only for one generation. The children born to the voluntary members of the first generation begin to make the sect a church long before they have arrived at the years of discretion. For with their coming the sect must take on the character of an educational and disciplinary institution, with the purpose of bringing the new generation into conformity with ideals and customs which have become traditional. Rarely does a second generation hold the convictions it has inherited with a fervor equal to that of its fathers, who fashioned these convictions in the heat of conflict and at the risk of martyrdom.[1]

The Covenant "Mystique"

While change is inevitable, despite the eagerness to recover an earlier fervor, the vision born in the mission house on Jefferson Street continues to inform and inspire our search for identity in this time and place. Karl Olsson called it "the Covenant mystique," which he sees as both our strength and our weakness: "The loyalty is not to a structure but to a mystique which flows from its understanding of itself as a non-creedal life movement, a family in the faith. The life-movement is centered in the living Christ and the faith and theology of the Covenant are nourished and directed by its devotion to the Bible."[2]

The strength of who we are lies in the profound sense of family, of being connected, so that wherever Covenanters meet there is an immediate sense of identity and belonging. Its weakness lies in what Olsson refers to as "a fierce and sometimes uncritical family loyalty, a sort of parochialism," which can also exclude.

The New Challenge

From this author's love affair with the Covenant, including Salem and its story, one is tempted to retreat into nostalgia for simpler times, for the uncluttered honesty and passionate faith of the forebears, and for the "first fine, careless rapture." With the passing of an intimate community defined by a single neighborhood on "this side of the river" and a church of the warm, open, trusting type, the new challenge confronting Salem, as I perceive it, is one of supplementing and contrasting the church as a family affair with what one author calls "the strong public image of the church as a company of strangers engaged in an evangelical conversation and life on behalf of the world."[3] More than making the stranger feel at home, it is the opening of one's own private, intimate world to the stranger, listening to the stranger, but also inviting all strangers into an open fellowship of justice, equality, and love—a place where Christ is present in word and sacrament and in the least of those who are members of his family (Matthew 25:40).

This, indeed, was in many ways the church of the immigrants, a company of strangers and resident aliens, seeking a safe place in their struggle for survival. The burden of their message was so important that they painted it on the wall of the mission house: "Behold the Lamb of God who takes away the sins of the world" (John 1:29). The inviting word of the gospel was symbolized by pail and dipper in the entry way of the mission house: "Come, ye who thirst." It was also the message to the woman crying out her lostness in the church balcony, and the preacher addressing her personally: "You are lost no longer. Your heavenly Father comes out to meet you."

Thus, the new challenge facing the church in a different time and place is not too dissimilar from the one facing an immigrant community. For this reason, the story of Salem needs retelling. But then it follows that the remembrance and custodial care of Salem's story lies in the retelling of the greater gospel story to the coming generation. This has been the reason for Salem's vitality through a hundred years and more. While change is inevitable, the good news remains the same: "Come, all ye who are weary and heavy laden." The table is spread for you, for all who will come!

Endnotes

Preface

1. The statement was made to the author by Dr. F. Burton Nelson on one of his several visits to Salem.

2. The quote is taken from the talk given at Salem in September 1991 by Austin Frisk.

Chapter 1
A Church Seeking Its Identity

1. Eric G. Hawkinson, trans., and Lois Bowman Michaelson, ed., *Son of the People: The Autobiography of C.V. Bowman* (Chicago: Covenant Publications, 1988). Bowman states, "In clothing, people of that day were much like today's children, following more or less the goddess of fashion. However, most of the Swedes were poor and were so recently arrived in America that they could not compete with the Americans and the aristocracy in general. Yet they were not completely 'separated from the world'" (p. 95).

2. Swedish Mission Tabernacle Congregation, *A Twenty-Five Year Memorial* (issued at the Jubilee, Minneapolis, Minnesota, October 29 to November 5, 1899). In this anniversary booklet, Rev. Gustaf E. Törnquist is described as a steady, calm personality, a richly endowed minister, an energetic worker who did not spare himself, and a person highly respected in the congregation and larger community. He was interested in the poor among whom he lived and was actively involved. On April 30, 1882, he passed away after a brief illness; he was buried in Lakewood Cemetery.

3. The phrase "few and poor" *(få och fattiga)* is the title of chapter 1 in *Images in Covenant Beginnings*, by Eric G. Hawkinson (Chicago: Covenant Press, 1968). The chapter begins as follows: "At the celebration of the fortieth anniversary of the Covenant church in Princeton, Illinois, Charles G. Swanson said, 'I can hardly speak today. My emo-

tions overwhelm me. When we started the work here, we were poor and few, but we sought the guidance of God in earnest prayers. He has blessed our efforts. The Holy Spirit has been in our midst, and sinners have been converted'" (p. 23). This calls to mind the hymn by Lina Sandell that might have been sung by the few gathered on Monroe Street:

> "Poor, but rich withal is Christ's chosen one;
> Poor within herself, rich in him alone;
> Poor in earthly goods, rich in Jesus' blood."

Translation by Karl A. Olsson, found in *New Hymns and Translations* (Chicago: Covenant Press, n.d.).

4. Philip J. Anderson, *A Precious Heritage: A Century of Mission in the Northwest 1884-1984* (Minneapolis: Northwest Conference, 1984), p. 8.

5. On September 14, 1888, a celebration took place commemorating the first Swedish settlement in America in New Sweden, Delaware. Hans Mattson appears to have been the initiator of the event and was its presiding officer, who also delivered the welcome address. It was held in the Exposition Building located on the east end of the Third Avenue bridge and was attended by some fifteen thousand people, many of whom stood for three hours. The Honorable W.W. Thomas, Jr., of Maine, former minister to Sweden and Norway, delivered the oration, in which he paid the following tribute to the immigrants:

> Everywhere they are noted for their honesty and thrift. Our Swedish settlers live within their means, buy no faster than they can pay, and do not run in debt. No other foreign race learn our language so quickly, or speak it so correctly and free from foreign accent, and none, I think, so speedily embrace our American ideas and become so thoroughly assimilated with us, and so completely Americanized. (This could be said, of course, about many other immigrant groups.)

Hans Mattson, *Souvenir: 250th Anniversary of the First Swedish Settlement in America* (Minneapolis, compiled and published by authority of the Committee, 1889).

6. The first movement for the territorial organization of Minnesota was made in the 1846-47 session of Congress. General H.H. Selby was elected to a seat in the House of Representatives on January 15, 1849, by a vote of 124 to 62. On March 3, 1849, Minnesota became a territory. In May of 1858 Minnesota was admitted into the Union and General Selby became the first governor. From the *Illustrated Historical Atlas of the State of Minnesota* (Chicago: A.I. Andreas, 1874).

7. F.L. Palmer, "In the Early Days and Now," *The East Side Argus*, Anniversary Edition, June 18, 1926.

8. Ibid.

9. Dingman's Grocery Store was located on the northeast corner of Lowry and Central Avenue (then known as Harrison Street and 25th Avenue). In the *Argus*, May 20, 1893, the following was reported: "G.L. Dingman, the pioneer grocer . . . has the past week

procedure, since the first meeting had not strictly conformed to the laws of the state of Minnesota regarding the number and term of the trustees.

Chapter 2
From Mission House to Tabernacle

1. This understanding of place is developed in *Landscapes of the Sacred,* by Belden C. Lane (New York: Paulist Press, 1988).

2. Skogsbergh refers to himself as "bishop of the churches," and rightly so. It remains a sourceof wonder that he could have been so ubiquitous in his interests and work. Pastor Carl Sandstrom's comment expressed this wonder: "He who bore the greatest burdens of trouble for the work during the time (leading up to the organization of the congregation) was, as we understand, Pastor Skogsbergh. How his time and energy could suffice to uphold the work and busy activities in the Mission House at 4th Street and 8th Avenue, and at the same time build the large tabernacle and have supervision of an outreach station in Northeast, north and south! This is more than we can understand." C.F. Sandstrom, *Minnesskrift*, 6.

3. The dimensions reported in the anniversary book were thirty-six by fifty feet, and the building permit indicates that the contractor was E.G. Erickson. We have drawn the conclusion that this most likely was the congregation's first chairman, A.G. Erickson.

4. Anderson, *A Precious Heritage,* 25, 26. August Bryngelson had a long career as a circuit rider in both Minnesota and Wisconsin, and was very active in Isanti, Chisago, and Kanabeck counties. Like the Apostle Paul, these itinerant preachers supported themselves with a trade and gave themselves generously and tirelessly to their preaching, fired by the conviction that the immigrant Swedes needed to be evangelized. This description by Philip Anderson includes a quotation from Karl Olsson:

> They rode their horses along wretched tracks; they jounced on newly laid rails; they slept in barns and stables and the most primitive shanties and mud huts; they held services in kitchens, under the open sky, in schoolhouses, and in scores of crude frame boxes called *missionshus*. Everywhere they went the hunger was the same. People wanted God.

In *Travel Memories from America 1876* (Chicago: Covenant Press, 1959), 87-88, C.J. Nyvall, traveling through the Midwest as a lay preacher from Sweden, makes the following observation:

> Preachers who would serve the Lord in America by seeking out the scattered immigrants must be prepared for serious privations. When I compare the circumstances here with those in Sweden I am convinced that many of our itinerant preachers at home would become less demanding and more satisfied with their lot, so far as lodging and such is concerned, if they had been in America for a time.

5. Swan W. Sundberg was the fourth pastor of the Swedish Evangelical Lutheran Mis-

sion Church of St. Paul (now First Covenant), from 1886-1897. He was vice-chairman at the organizational meeting of the Covenant in February of 1885, and an outstanding preacher and leader for many years.

6. C.F. Sandstrom, *Minnesskrift*, 10.

7. In a letter written by Erick Lundquist to his family in Sweden, returned to relatives in America some seventy-five years later, one gets a glimpse into the spirit of the mission house on Jefferson Street. The letter, including the following excerpt dated January 18, 1891, was translated by Erick's granddaughter, Vernice Monson. It was written to Erick Abrahamson, Lundquist's father-in-law.

> Grace and Peace from our God: A year has passed . . . and once again I want to greet you. Time passes so quickly. It is now soon four years since we left our dear parents and brothers and sisters that we truly thought we would never see again before we meet at that great judgment day before Christ's throne. But as time passes one ponders many times the question—"How are you?" I think that thought is more evident for those that are apart from their homeland and more from their dear loved ones. In the meantime, time flies and we are nearer our true and only home. That shall be a blessed meeting when we meet there at home to rest. Oh, that none of our family may be missing there. . . .
>
> Prayer week which we have had for two weeks is now over. Large crowds have left their hearts with Jesus. Prayer and petition, praise and thanksgiving has arisen. Praise His Name! I cannot with this dead pen describe what a blessed time we have had. I feel much more thankful to God for the benefit of having God's peace in my heart and joy in the Holy Spirit. That is a daily quest. How much more then shall we enjoy that to the fullest at God's right hand in eternity. . . .
>
> I hope you will write a little through someone and tell about how you are and how it is on that spiritual journey and at the home place. Finally, the Lord be with us and you all. Greet all acquaintances and relatives. Especially, you are heartily greeted by
>
> Erick Lundquist and your daughter, Amanda

8. These materials were received from personal interviews.

9. C.F. Sandstrom, *Minnesskrift*, 14.

10. Aaron Carlson purchased the mission house on Jefferson Street for $1,500 and converted it into an apartment complex. In the seventy-fifth anniversary book, *Footsteps in Faith* (1963), the observation is made that during the ministry of Rev. August Sjoberg (1893-1900) "only three men in the church were prosperous enough to own horses and buggies," Aaron Carlson, John Olson, and August Anderson. These three along with the church chairman, Gustaf August Erickson, became the search committee and eventually the building committee for the new tabernacle.

11. E.A. Skogsbergh was an amateur architect who designed the Swedish Tabernacles (now First Covenant) in Minneapolis and Seattle, Washington. He is reported to have

said that he designed the pillars large enough so that timid sinners might have a place to hide! Pastor Hjalmar Sundquist designed the Tabernacle in St. Paul, inspired by the Mormon Tabernacle in Salt Lake City, but on a much smaller scale.

12. Hjalmar Sundquist (1869-1949) was the fifth pastor of First Covenant, St. Paul. When the Tabernacle was dedicated on May 11, 1902, Pastor Sundquist delivered his first address in English, part of which is quoted above.

13. Karl A. Olsson, *By One Spirit* (Chicago: Covenant Press, 1962), 519.

14. Bowman, *Son of the People*, 218.

15. Minutes of the business meeting of the Swedish Evangelical Mission Church of Northeast Minneapolis, held September 30, 1901.

Chapter 3
From Tabernacle to Church

1. This reflection piece appeared in the Salem Covenant newsletter in 1970.

2. Calvin Anderson at a book-taping interview, February 20, 1990. Several of the following memories were shared in similar interviews conducted by the history committee.

3. Ronald Johnson.

4. Kathleen Morford. She also recalls a chow mein dinner prepared in the kitchen of the church on Central Avenue where the sticky rice grew until there was rice all over the place.

5. Marion Hagman, "Recollections of Earlier Days at Salem," 1986.

6. Jerome Green at the funeral of his aunt, Olga Gustafson.

7. Mark Stohlberg

8. Dorothy Lundstrom Balch, "A View from the '20's and '30's of Salem Saints and Sunday School Teachers," September 1994.

9 . Ibid.

10. Ibid.

11. Marlys and Rick Sjoblom at the baptism of their son, Mark.

12. Hagman, "Recollections of Earlier Days."

13. Balch, "A View . . . of Salem Saints."

14. Ibid.

15. The story belongs to Salem's oral history and has wide circulation throughout the Covenant. Bill Goolsbee, chairman at the time of Pastor Clarence Agard's farewell, did not intentionally choose the hymn but announced the wrong number by mistake.

16. Glen Bjorklund. "Those were very interesting days, and difficult between us all. There were two sides that were starting to form. . . . One group felt there was a real need to move and of course, another group who said there was no need to go. God intended us to be here and we should stay here to serve the people of the community. . . . Then we got down to the final vote that night which way we should go. . . . Our decisions seemed to get easier and easier as time went along. That's the thing that really sticks out in my mind."

17. Calvin Anderson in the same book-taping session expressed his own ambiguous feelings as a young person during that time: "I never really understood the complexities of the old church crumbling. I always thought that the church should stay there. I was disappointed as a youngster, because all the hiding places and the good humor that went with the old church we were now leaving and going to some place completely strange. As people look back from a sentimental point of view, I realize how attached we were. But I understand now that there were good reasons why we had to leave."

18. In material prepared for a vignette celebrating Salem's centennial, Laurie Peterson made this observation: "In another effort to reach out into the community a program called Friendship Evangelism was begun wherein we sought to invite people in the neighborhood into our homes. It seemed that there was a definite economic barrier because that neighborhood was comprised more and more of people of lower income and an increasing number of single mothers who were on welfare. Our parish worker, Olga Gustafson, carried on a very active home visitation program and kept records of her calls. Card after card in her files would show that six months after a previous visit, many of these single mothers and others who had bettered themselves economically had moved from the community. As a result Sunday School attendance also declined."

19. Recollections of that crucial meeting by many who were there speak of two factors that seemed to turn the tide: the presence of so many young people whose futures were at stake in the decision, and the persuasive, well-chosen words of Dora Johnson, a gifted, articulate laywomen in the congregation.

20. The Executive Building Council was comprised of the following:

Co-chairmen: Harold Lundeen and Glen Bjorklund
Survey: David Borgstrom
Christian Education: Paul V. Anderson
Furnishings and Equipment: Norman Engman
Administration and Facilities: Laurie Peterson

Fellowship and Recreation: Bernard Bengtson
Finance: Harlan Erickson
Memorial Gifts: Norman Hoglund
Plans and Construction: Curtiss D. Johnson
Publicity: Homer Eclov

21. A lengthy period of negotiations with the housing authority began with their original offer for the Central Avenue property of $170,000, including $9,000 for a house next to the church, $13,500 for a duplex on Polk Street, and $17,429 for personal property. This offer was rejected by the congregation. An earlier offer of $100,000 for the property had been made by the Minneapolis Revival Mission. Concern by church members and some merchants on Central Avenue was expressed, and the offer was declined. The city's interest in the property was for building a housing complex for seniors, and a senior citizen high-rise now stands on the ground of old Salem.

22. Evelyn Strand recalls that "there were times when we would come to church and find a little pile of plaster in the middle of a room which had fallen from the ceiling."

23. The story was told by Al Ryd.

24. The story was told by Laurie Peterson for one of the vignettes during the centennial year. He was chairman of the congregation at the time.

25. The tribute to lay leadership would be incomplete without reference to the chairmen who served during this critical period of transition: Ward Holm, Laurie Peterson, and Norman Engman.

26. Erik Dahlhielm, *A Burning Heart* (Chicago: Covenant Press, 1951), 3.

27. Quoted in "Go Forward . . . A 90th Year Reflection of Salem Covenant Church," 1978.

Chapter 4
A Story of Caretakers

1. Ole Rölvaag, *The Third Life of Per Smevik* (New York: Harper and Row, 1971), 105.

2. Sometime later a fourth district was added to include the Columbia Heights area. In September of 1961 the evangelism committee of Salem launched a denominational program called Under-Shepherding as a friendship plan in which the parish was divided into smaller zones. This would have been nothing new to the earlier three-district plan.

3. A.G. Erickson eventually moved to California and settled in Kingsburg.

4. An extraordinary story in many ways in that John K. Merricks was a charter member of the Swedish Lutheran Mission Church in St. Paul and then in Minneapolis (now

First Covenant), and joined the mission house at 17th and Jefferson Street shortly after its organization. He was the manager of a furniture and undertaking establishment, and served as the first organist of the congregation.

5. Driving north on Highway 100 one can see the sign "John Martin Drive," named after this person who gave Aaron Carlson his beginning. John Martin was also the grandfather of Earle Brown, who became sheriff of Hennepin County and ran unsuccessfully against Floyd Olson for governor.

6. There was a popular saying among the immigrants that "you worked at Aaron Carlson's, bought clothes at Ecklund's and hardware at Billman's."

7. Bowman, *Son of the People*, 222. In an interview on February 1, 1993, Robert G. Anderson, who lives on Turtle Lake and knows its history, said that Aaron Carlson owned a steamboat—the only one he has ever heard of being on Turtle Lake. "Someone was telling me that the wood carvers who worked on the Swedish Institute—he would allow to go fishing if they took their carving with them and worked on it in the boat. . . . Of course, the wood carvers got more money than the rest. They were specialists."

8. Ibid, 218. In the Aaron Carlson story, mention must be made of Aaron's wife, Minnie. She was born on February 17, 1860, in the same parish as Aaron, Västra Fågelvik, Värmland, Sweden, the daughter of Lars and Anna Halvorson. Because of her father's name, Lars, her maiden name was Minnie Larson. Aaron Carlson and Minnie Larson were married on March 18, 1885, in Minneapolis, a year before Aaron joined the mission house on Jefferson Street. Despite Aaron's active role in Salem, Minnie never joined the congregation. According to Edith Lundeen, a relative and long-standing member of Salem, she did not join Salem because she was so fond of the preaching of Rev. A.E. Palmquist, pastor of the Swedish Tabernacle (now First Covenant) in St. Paul. She is also remembered by Salem members for owning one of the first electric cars in Minneapolis, and for her gracious hospitality in entertaining guests both on Hayes Street and in their home at Turtle Lake. Minnie died on December 24, 1938, followed by Aaron on November 24, 1942. Both are buried in Lakewood Cemetery, Minneapolis.

9. The story of lay participation in the Vietnamese Refugee Sponsorship Committee is truly inspiring, both in the numbers of people involved and in the response to needs as these were identified. The focus groups were as follows: Housing Search, Clothing, Furnishings, Medical, Dental, Job Search, Food, English Tutoring, Education, Friendship, Transportation, Airport, Official Welcome Party, Legal, and Weekly Shopping.

10. Frank Lunquist has made available his extensive record of all the Vietnamese persons with whom the congregation has had contact. The tape recorded interviews made by Bill Plice with Lan Nguyen and Chanh Vo are also available in the archives.

11. Ibid.

Chapter 5
A Gospel-centered Church

1. The centennial banners were created by LaVonne Ecker and Sharon Walker, who are both members of Salem.

2. Vera Jernall, in an interview, tells of a family living across the street from them who always got water from the Jernall well. When their home was quarantined they would leave their water pail in the center of the street and the Jernalls would bring water and pour into it. Vera also spoke of the water pail at the church and commented that she didn't care to drink from it after watching some of the "mustached, tobacco-chewing men" drink from the dipper.

3. Dahlhielm, *A Burning Heart*, 3-4. J. M. Sanngren came to Chicago in 1868, and until 1876 he served the first Covenant church to be established in the city. He became president of the Mission Synod in 1873 and served in that position until his death in 1878.

4. David H. Sandstrom, *Landmarks of the Spirit* (New York: Pilgrim Press, 1985), 28.

5. Paul LeRoy Holmer, "The Grammar of Faith," in *The Grammar of the Heart*, ed. Richard H. Bell (San Francisco: Harper and Row, 1988), 15. What Holmer says about teaching applies to preaching as well. What is required is to " insulate the listener into a new role; the listener's self evaluation, subjectivity, aims, wishes, hopes, desires must be altered so that the grammar of faith becomes relevant. When the right supposal envelopes her, when she understands herself to be a prisoner, a victim, a sinner, a changeling, then the teachings will come to life so that the hearers will discover their place, opportunities, and possibilities anew."

6. In *A Twenty-Five Year Memorial*, Skogsbergh speaks of the Swedish Tabernacle as besieged from without by "partisan exploiters who sought to produce discord and division. If Minneapolis had been a place chosen of God for mighty works, it now appeared to have become an area for partisan strife and disunity with the intent to harm and ruin God's work" (14).

7. Bowman, *Son of the People*, 220-221.

8. C. A. Gavert, ed., *Minnesskrift 1888-1928 Historisk över Svenska Missionsförsamlingen Salem* (A History of the Swedish Mission congregation Salem) (Minneapolis: 1928). The Swedish language certainly did not protect congregations from extremes, as indicated by the footnote above. But fortunately, Salem was spared from discord and division within.

9. Olsson, *By One Spirit*, 520.

10. Paul L. Holmer, "Salem Days," *Covenant Companion*, June 30, 1967. Paul Holmer grew up in Salem; he wrote this article at the time he was professor of theology at Yale University Divinity School in New Haven, Connecticut.

11. This story was told by Clarence Nelson as president of the Covenant in a personal telephone call to Rev. Wallace H. Pratt when he was going through a difficult time as a young pastor of a West Coast Covenant church.

12. The sermon was preached on July 24, 1977.

13. From a sermon, "The Church with the Pail and Dipper Says 'Come'!" preached by Pastor Glen V. Wiberg on the first Sunday opening Salem's centennial year, January 3, 1988.

Chapter 6
A Worshiping Church

1. *A Book of Worship for Covenant Churches* (Chicago: Covenant Press, 1964), xxiii.

2. Ibid., xxi, xxvi.

3. Ibid., xxvi. The concluding words are memorable: "All careless, objectionable, or ridiculous matters should be far removed from 'the beautiful worship of the Lord.' The people which shall at one time come forth in shining white garments and live in a city of gold and precious stones should even on earth diligently seek to appear in a worthy and gracious manner" (Philippians 4:8).

4. Hawkinson, *Images in Covenant Beginnings,* 86.

5. *Evangelii Basun* (The Gospel Trumpet) was a joint project of Rev. E. August Skogsbergh and A.L. Skoog. The 1894 edition contained 563 hymns with a supplement of 50 hymn-anthems for the choir. *Sionsharpan* (Zion's Harp) was published in 1890 by the Mission Friends Publishing Company of Chicago and edited by Nils Frykman, David Nyvall, and Fridolf Risberg. It contained 700 hymns and had the advantage of being arranged according to title and content.

6. The string band continued for a number of years following the move to Central Avenue. During the ministry of Rev. C. A. Gavert, Mrs. Gavert led the string band. According to Marion Hagman, a long-time member of Salem, the young people referred to the string band as "Mrs. Gavvy's Syncopators." During the early 1930s, C.H. Kjellberg, who served as Sunday school superintendent for two terms and as church custodian, led the string band, which included women. The group played for special occasions and often traveled to other churches. On the occasion of the ninetieth anniversary of the congregation the string band was revived, consisting of Paul V. Anderson, Orville Bjorklund, Norman Hoglund, Kennison Frith, Paul Peterson, Richard Sjoblom, Gary Schwartz, Dennis Schwartz, Tim Schwartz, and Lester Schwartz, who was the leader. The group continues to give concerts in churches, retirement homes, and church events and has produced two cassettes, "Songs of Praise" (1990) and "Sing His Praise" (1993).

7. Holmer, "Salem Days," 4.

8. David H. Sandstrom, *Landmarks of the Spirit*, 26-28. A description of C.F. Sandstrom's preaching style is given in the previous chapter.

9. The debt Salem owes to its choir directors and organists is immense. A list of musicians is found in the appendices.

10. The first pipe organ built by George Kilgen and Son was a two-manual pneumatic organ consisting of three divisions: the great organ, the swell organ, and the pedal organ. The organ was rebuilt with the help of a consultant, Harry Iverson, and dedicated on January 3, 1943. The instrument was electrified, usable sections of the old organ were retained and improved, new ranks of pipes were added, and the console with a redesigned organ case was installed on the platform. Guest organist for the rededication was C. Wesley Andersen.

11. *Sions Basun* was the first official hymnal of the Covenant and was similar in content to *Sionsharpan*. It consisted of 704 Swedish hymns and 27 English hymns. The committee which produced the hymnal consisted of a triumvirate of musicians: Nils Frykman, A.L. Skoog, and J.A. Hultman, together with four pastors: J.J. Daniels, Albert W. Johanson, F.M. Johnson, and A.G. Sporrong. A small hymnal, *Sions Glädjebud* (Zion's Joyous Message), was used for a short time at Salem. It was edited by J.J. Daniels, a Covenant pastor in Minneapolis. It was published in 1904 and contained 262 hymns, 62 of which were designated as choir and solo songs. Guitar chords were also provided.

12. In the business meeting of September 3, 1937, which set the date of the dedication of the communion table and baptismal font, Pastor Clarence A. Nelson was authorized to use the silver chalice from the old communion ware in the celebration of Holy Communion. Another indication of the priesthood of the congregation!

13. The organ built by Hillgren, Lane and Company of Alliance, Ohio, was a two-manual organ with pedal keyboard consisting of 979 pipes. It was dedicated on January 31, 1960, with D. Byron Arneson as guest organist, one of the builders of the organ. The comment was made in the dedicatory program that the manual keys were imported from England and had extra-thick ivories!

14. Patricia Hampl, *Virgin Time* (New York: Farrar, Straus and Giroux, 1992), 195.

15. Salem newsletter, April 1, 1971.

16. "The Eye Brow Window," which is forty-six feet long and six feet high, was designed by a noted artist, Dieter Spahn, who was born in Dusseldorf, Germany. According to the artist, the window is intended to show the constant change of life, with the further intent that "every person could interpret the meaning for himself." The glass imported from Germany was cut, each piece painted, then fired in a kiln and leaded according to the design.

17. In the remodeling of the chancel in preparation for the installation of the new organ in 1987, the broad and spacious communion table was made into a free-standing

table more in keeping with the tradition of the early Mission Friends.

18. The wood sculpture by Neale Murray was dedicated on All Saints' Day, November 1, 1981.

19. In a letter to Curtiss D. Johnson, January 20, 1994, Greg Carter responded to a request for some artistic explanations of the mural by the artist himself:

> The introductory passage begins at the entrance of the room with a veiled female figure in front of the earth being formed out of void. This is the beginning, the first day of creation. . . . Beside that is the creation of man in a stylized version of Michelangelo's Sistine Chapel painting. This rounds the corner and enters in the main room which shows the contemporary world as I see it. These images do not tell a story together; they are individual impressions of a young person trying to make sense out of the world. From the far left sunlight streams down through redwood trees dwarfing the people below (this speaks of scale, the immensity of creation and the smallness of humans, trying to show a sense of wonder at humanity's small perspective). The quote by Betti suggests that we should be open to experiencing "wonderful surprises". . . . Below the quote is the flip side of the coin, human suffering. This image of suffering is very close to a crucifixion scenario. . . . Beside the crucifixion and overlapping it is my silhouette with streams of light from the redwood scene crossing through my form. Beside the quote is a NASA shot of the earth from space (again this talks about scale, universe vs. earth vs. one individual). Beside the earth is another silhouette of me; this time standing with demon eyes from the right panel (this says that I have both the good symbolized by the streaming light and the bad symbolized by the demon eyes inside of me.) Beside this full figure outline are two hands (scale again: big vs. small, age vs. youth, wonder of the coexistence of such different things). Beside the hands are . . . the men in suits who were good men but who made bad decisions, had used their God-given free will for the wrong ends. Instead of appreciating wonder in life and acting accordingly, they had created the pain and suffering that now fill the world. In the process they had lost the ability to tell the difference between the good and the bad, hence the quote below the glaring heads by the rock band Pink Floyd. The heads blend back into the Michelangelo creation image and the Crucified.

20. The paraments were created by Shirley Herrick, a member of St. Philip's Lutheran Church, Fridley, Minnesota, and Bonnie Johnson Nelson, a former member of Salem and now a member of First Covenant Church, Seattle, Washington. The permanent banner, which is sixteen feet long and four feet two inches wide, was designed by Erland Ekberg, Jr., an architect, and was handcrafted by Marjorie Ford, a fiber artist.

21. The Holtkamp Organ was designed by Walter Holtkamp of Cleveland, Ohio, in consultation with John Ferguson, professor of church music at St. Olaf College in Northfield, Minnesota, and the Organ Committee of Salem. The organ is composed of four divisions: the great organ, the swell organ, the solo organ, and the pedal organ. In total the organ has forty-two ranks of pipes, organized as thirty-two stops. There are 2,243 pipes in the organ, running from a length of less than one inch up to sixteen

feet in length. John Ferguson was the guest organist in a service of lessons and music on September 20, 1987. Later a Yamaha concert grand piano was given by the family of Clinton W. Stark in his memory, thereby enhancing the musical possibilities for worship.

22. C.F. Sandstrom's comment about Skogsberg in his *Minnesskrift,* 11.

23. A phrase from Patricia Hampl's *Virgin Time*, cited above.

Chapter 7
Women With Names

1. Originally, women did not have the right to vote at congregational meetings. On January 1, 1898, the minutes contain this entry: "A motion was made that at a suitable time the question be considered as to the right-to-vote of the women in the congregation." However, there is no indication in minutes that follow that the issue was considered. When the constitution was printed in 1911, the matter had apparently been resolved. Under Article 1, "Membership," it states in part 4 that "every member has the right to speak and vote at all congregational meetings."

2. The Missions Fellowship Group of Covenant Women meets on the second Tuesday of the month for sewing and fellowship. Phyllis Ryd is presently the leader.

3. Britta was the mother of Olof Olsson (1841-1900), who founded the Bethany Lutheran Church in Lindsborg, Kansas, in the 1860s. He was a long-time friend of Carl Johan Nyvall (1829-1904), and was characterized by Karl Olsson as "a warm-hearted evangelical who never quite reconciled himself to the confessional rigidity of the Augustana Synod" (Olsson, *By One Spirit,* 210).

4. Those interested in this fascinating story should seek out two books of immense importance, *Travel Memories from America 1876,* by C. J. Nyvall, trans. E. Gustav Johnson (Chicago: Covenant Press, 1959), and *My Father's Testament*, by David Nyvall, trans. Eric G. Hawkinson (Chicago: Covenant Press, 1974).

5. The society was originally for single women. Single girls who married could continue as members, but women already married could not join. The story is told about Beatrice Holm, who had to hurry and join Chen King U while she was still Beatrice Hedsten. On December 8, 1942, the first amendment to the constitution was changed so that married women could be accepted as members of the society.

6. The artist who created the two centennial stained glass panels is Jeff Swenson, of Swenson Art Glass, Minneapolis.

7. Olsson, *By One Spirit*, 454-455.

8. This story was related to me by Blanche Nelson, wife of Clarence A. Nelson.

9. Such words of tribute were spoken at the memorial service held for Martha on January 18, 1948. *The Covenant Weekly* for March 19, 1948, contained this report:

> On Sunday afternoon, January 18, a church filled to capacity witnessed the memorial service held in Martha's honor. President T.W. Anderson, Rev. Ralph P. Hanson, Rev. Clarence A. Nelson, and to represent the country Martha loved and for which she gave herself, Dr. Peng Fu (president of the Lutheran Church of China) and Miss Clara Jones (Lutheran missionary to China and personal friend of Martha who translated Dr. Peng Fu's message into English). The Rev. Clarence D. Agard, pastor of the church, was in charge of the service, and spoke words of comfort to the beloved family. Mrs. Richard Swanson sang "Rock of Ages," song of Martha's choice and Mrs. Swanson and Mr. Helmer Statine sang two hymns, "As He Wills" and "Precious Hiding Place." The audience joined in the singing of A.L. Skoog's beautiful hymn, "The Day of Christ."

10. Alma Johnson was born in Västergötland, Sweden, on September 29, 1879, daughter of Louis Johnson and Lotta Swenson. In September of 1903 the weekday school committee reported that it was able to secure "a very good and able teacher, Alma Elvira Johnson." When she was called as church deaconess in 1913 at a salary of forty dollars a month, her work was varied and far-reaching. Her first report was as follows: eighteen weeks nursing care, 253 house calls, 103 sick calls in homes, 27 in hospitals, 115 bouquets of flowers donated and delivered, taught Swedish weekday school for six weeks, served as delegate to the young people's conference in Duluth. She is described in an earlier anniversary book as "a sort of general assistant to all; since she lived next door to the church, anyone wanting access got the key at her home." She lived at 1819 Central Avenue until her death on February 28, 1946.

George Bergquist pays tribute to Alma Johnson as "the person who best symbolizes what Salem Church meant to me from the very beginning," then tells the following story: "I recall that she visited us one afternoon, and Mother, wanting to show her how much little George had learned in her call, asked me to tell Alma Johnson the story of the mustard seed. In the pattern of little boys who resist being asked to perform, I replied, 'I've never heard of it'—though I knew the answer perfectly well. Alma Johnson smiled and understood. She, together with other female and male Alma Johnsons, made Salem a secure haven of love, devotion and Christian teaching" (May 1994).

Chapter 8
Telling the Next Generation, Part I

1. Karl A. Olsson, "Covenant Beginnings: Communal," 75, 76. See also "The Mystical and Corporate Nature of the Covenant Church," by Karl A. Olsson, in *The Covenant Quarterly*, vol. 18, no. 4 (November 1985), 11.

2. *A Book of Worship for Covenant Churches*, 56, 57.

3. *Ett Tjugufemårsminne* (*Twenty-five Year Anniversary Booklet*) indicates that in 1882, six years before the congregation was organized, "a pair of brothers who belonged to the

Tabernacle congregation started a work among the children. The numbers were not so large, only about seven, and the teaching was in the homes. Of these little seeds have grown up a truly considerable tree" (23). Frans Larson had an active role in the early beginnings of the Sunday school, followed by L.M. Lindquist, who was superintendent for twenty-seven years.

4. Translated by Vernice Monson from the minutes of the Swedish Evangelical Mission Church, page 162, written on behalf of the Sunday school by Gustaf N. Ohlson, secretary.

5. Marion Hagman, "Recollections of Earlier Days at Salem," 1986. Following her death on February 4, 1988, a lecture series, "The Marion R. Hagman Scholar-In-Residence Program," was established by her family in tribute to Marion, who was a deeply loyal lifetime member of Salem. As a disciple of Christ, she lived with a faith always on the growing edge. Since the program's inauguration, lecturers have included Paul L. Holmer (1992); a panel of artists: Thomas Becknell in American literature, Stewart Luckman in sculpture, Don Postema in film, and Wayne Roosa in art history (1993); Mary Ellen Ashcroft (1994); and Thomas Green (1995).

6. Personal recollections of the Salem Church by George W. Bergquist, May 19, 1994. A native of Minneapolis, George earned bachelor and graduate degrees at Harvard in government and economics. After service in the Navy as an officer in World War II, he had a long career in financial management in the Department of Defense. He was knighted by King Carl Gustaf XVI of Sweden with the Royal Order of the North Star for helping the Swedish defense ministry develop a new planning and budgeting system. He has been an active member of the New York Avenue Presbyterian Church in Washington, D.C., since 1952.

7. Karl A. Olsson, *Into One Body*, vol. 2 (Chicago: Covenant Press, 1986), 285.

8. Minutes of the Swedish Evangelical Mission Church of Northeast Minneapolis, January 1, 1906, 81.

9. Ibid, 113. Several teachers for the Swedish day school were recruited from North Park College. Among them were Renius Johnson, Alma Johnson, Henning Peterson, and Ture E. Nordberg, whose report for the annual meeting for 1905 is quoted.

10. Olsson, *Into One Body*, 242.

11. Erik Dahlhielm, "Half A Century in the Fellowship of the Gospel," in *After Fifty Years: A Resumé of the Development and Service of the Salem Swedish Mission Church, Minneapolis, Minnesota 1888-1938*.

12. Some of the more recent themes used in the 1980s for daily vacation Bible school were: "Sonseeker Safari," "Share the Good News," "Sonlight Mountain," and "God's Champions." The amount of time, energy, staffing, and creativity invested in a single week has been remarkable. It continues to be a significant ministry of community outreach in telling the old, old story.

13. Rev. Craig Nelson, who served as president of Minnehaha Academy from 1977 to 1994, is the son of Rev. and Mrs. Clarence A. Nelson and was baptized at Salem.

14. Minutes cited above, January 1, 1906, 82.

Chapter 9
Telling the Next Generation, Part II

1. The letter was written by Nellie Lundquist (Nelson) to her cousin Gottfrid Larsson in Värmland, Sweden. Nellie was eighteen years of age at the time. She was later married to Oscar A. Nelson and was the mother of Waldo Nelson and Jeanette Nelson Schwartz. This letter is one of many letters written by family member to relatives in Sweden and seventy-five years later returned to the Lundquist family. All of these letters, translated by Vernice Monson, reflect immigrant life at that time.

2. Donald C. Frisk (1911-) was ordained by the Swedish Evangelical Mission Covenant in June of 1936 in Duluth, Minnesota. While serving the Covenant Congregational Church in New Rochelle, New York, he pursued further theological studies at Union Seminary, New York. He spent a year at the Swedish Mission Covenant Seminary in Lidingö, Sweden, from 1938 to 1939. Returning from Sweden, he served the Mission Covenant Church in Princeton, Illinois. In 1945 he was called to teach systematic theology at North Park Seminary, where, upon the retirement of Eric G. Hawkinson, he served as dean of the seminary for six years. He retired in 1978 and currently resides at The Holmstad in Batavia, Illinois.

3. Paul L. Holmer (1916-), upon earning his Ph.D. in philosophy from Yale University, returned to Minnesota to teach at Gustavus Adolphus College, St. Peter, and the University of Minnesota, where in 1954 he became full professor of philosophy. In 1960 he returned to Yale University as the Noah Porter Professor of Philosophical Theology. Since his retirement in 1987, he resides in Northeast Minneapolis, where he continues a rigorous schedule of teaching and preaching.

4. Salem Mission Young People's Society minutes book, page 26. The report was given by a member of the society, Olive Berg. She was the first woman from Salem to serve in the armed forces during World War II. Her married name was Magnus.

5. Minutes of the Swedish Evangelical Mission Church of Northeast Minneapolis, December 7, 1891.

6. Kendig Brubaker Cully, ed., *Confirmation: History, Doctrine and Practice* (Greenwich, Connecticut: Seabury Press, 1962), 37, 38.

7. Confirmation texts and authors are as follows:

The *Small Catechism* by Martin Luther
Kristlig Troslära, by Nils Frykman, Axel Mellander, and David Nyvall (1893)
The Christian Faith (a translation of the above in 1938)

Youth and the Way of Life, by Alfred J. Johnson, William Freeman, Carl G. Charn (1944)
According to Thy Word, by Clifford Bjorklund, Harry J. Ekstam, Karl A. Olsson, Donald C. Frisk (1954).
The Story of God's People (Year 1), by F. Burton Nelson (1971)
Called to Be His People (Year 2), by Glen V. Wiberg (1970)
God's Friends, by Wesley W. Nelson (1985)

8. Personal recollection of the Salem church by George W. Bergquist, May 19,1994.

9. Karl A. Olsson, *A Family of Faith* (Chicago: Covenant Press, 1975), 44. I have also been greatly helped in the more detailed chronology of David Nyvall's life by a draft of a doctoral thesis on Nyvall by Scott E. Erickson, Uppsala University, Sweden, May 30, 1994.

10. The budget for the preschool in 1994 was $71,920.

11. This philosophy of Salem's preschool stated by Pam Carlson has been the shared vision of its staff members: June Abrahamson, Kathy Dulitz, Judy Edlund, Liz Forestell, Kathie Frank, Myl Harris, Melba Holmberg, Ruth Hultgren, Kathy Johnson, Cathy Larson, Snella Lundin, Kathy Morford, Lynn Rees, Cheryl Roosa, Beth Sandell, Karen Scheibe, and Jan Swanson.

12. I am indebted to Walter Brueggeman's fine book *Biblical Perspectives on Evangelism* for the insights he has regarding the evangelical task of passing on the faith to the next generation.

Postscript

1. H. Richard Niebuhr, *The Social Sources of Denominationalism* (Hamden, Connecticut: The Shoe String Press, 1959), 19, 20.

2. Karl A. Olsson, *Into One Body*, vol. 2, 38. Regarding "the Covenant mystique," he says it may have been "too subtle to attract and hold the second generation. When they came under the influence of other communions, either more conservative or more liberal than the Covenant they found it all too easy to renounce a tradition which had made no great impact on them. . . . The 'feeling of family' was not strong enough to encourage them to stay and work through the difficult language and cultural transition" (70, 71).

3. Patrick R. Keifert, *Welcoming the Stranger: A Public Theology of Worship and Evangelism* (Minneapolis: Fortress Press, 1992), 90, 91.

Appendix A
Salem's Pastors

Organizing Pastor

Erik August Skogsbergh was born in Glava Parish, Värmland, Sweden, on June 24, 1850. Converted at the age of nineteen, he pursued studies for the ministry in Kristinehamn and Ahlsborg School, Vetlanda, Småland, and immigrated to America in 1876. On January 22, 1877, he was ordained by the Swedish Evangelical Lutheran Mission Synod in Princeton, Illinois. He was united in marriage to Mathilda S. Peterson on May 31, 1879, a union to which were born ten children and which lasted for more than fifty-one years. He served the Tabernacle church in Chicago and in 1884 became pastor of the Swedish Tabernacle (now First Covenant) in Minneapolis, where he served for twenty-five years. He founded a school in his church which was later to become North Park College, and was one of the founders of Minnehaha Academy. He established two newspapers, published hymnals, and engaged in other activities including the founding and chartering of the Swedish Evangelical Mission Church of Minneapolis (now Salem). Following his pastorate in Minneapolis, he accepted a call to the First Covenant Church of Seattle, where he designed and built the present church edifice as he had also done in Minneapolis. During the last twenty years of his life he was active as a traveling preacher and evangelist. He died in Minneapolis on October 31, 1939, at the age of eighty-nine years. For further reading see *A Burning Heart*, by Erik Dahlhielm.

Senior Pastors

A. G. Olson was assistant pastor at the Swedish Tabernacle and served as secretary of the organizational meeting of the Northeast congregation on December 17, 1888. He accepted the call to become the first pastor at the mission house on Jefferson Street, but served only a brief time from December 27, 1888, to May 1889, when, for undisclosed reasons, the Tabernacle called for his dismissal. No biographical information is known other than his death in Stockholm, Saskatchewan, Canada, in January of 1931.

Karl August Jonson was born in Sunnemo, Värmland, on February 8, 1852, and immigrated to America in 1880. During his early ministry he preached to settlers in the Red River Valley and later served the churches at Lund, Stockholm, River Falls, and Mann Valley, Wisconsin. Pastor Jonson served as secretary of the first mission association, which became the Northwest Conference, organized on October 27, 1884, at Pennock, Minnesota; and he attended the organizational meeting of the ministerium in June of 1885. On October 7, 1889, he was called to the Swedish Evangelical Mission Church (now Salem) and served until early in 1893. Remaining in Minneapolis, he became manager of Skogsbergh's paper, *Veckobladet* (The Weekly). During the final years of his life he was an itinerant preacher in various churches in Minnesota and Wisconsin. He died in Minneapolis on November 3, 1915, leaving his wife and four children: August Emmanuel, Paul, Ruth, and Vera. Biographical data relating to the dates of marriage and ordination are not known.

August Sjöberg was born on March 23, 1845, in the parish of Vreta, Västergötland. He began his ministerial career in Sweden, where he served as pastor for several years at Mariestad and as an itinerant preacher for the Västergötland Missionary Association. He was married to Charlotta Larson on May 30, 1875. In 1888 he immigrated to America. He served the Pilgrim church in Brooklyn, New York, and then the church at Ridgeway, Pennsylvania. On November 6, 1893, Pastor Sjöberg was called to the mission house on Jefferson Street, where he served until July 1, 1900. Following his years in Minneapolis, he served congregations at French Lake and Long Lake, Minnesota. He died at the home of his son, Dr. S.P. Seaberg, in Spokane, Washington, on May 2, 1920.

Carl Victor Bowman was born in the parish of Marbäck, Jönköpings län, Småland, Sweden, on June 13, 1868. As a young boy of nine years of age, he immigrated to America with three aunts, arriving in Chicago on October 3, 1879. In 1885 he was converted under the preaching of Rev. F.M. Johnson, pastor of the Tabernacle church, Chicago. On June 4, 1892, he was married to Julia Nelson. They had five children: Alpha, Earl, Carl, Malcolm, and Raymond. For one year he attended Skogsbergh's school in Minneapolis, then went to North Park, where he graduated from the seminary in 1896. He was ordained by the Swedish Evangelical Mission Covenant of America at its Annual Meeting at North Park in Chicago on June 3, 1897. Prior to his call to Salem on July 9, 1900, he served as pastor of the Tabernacle church of Chicago. During his seven-year pastorate at Salem, he also served from 1904 to 1907 as part-time superintendent of the Northwest Conference. Following his resignation from Salem on September 30, 1907, he served as the first full-time superintendent of the Northwest Conference until 1910. This was followed by pastorates at the Covenant Congregational Church, Boston, Massachusetts, and the Edgewater Covenant Church, Chicago. In 1920 he became the first secretary of missions for the denomination, and from 1927 to 1933 he served as the third president of the Swedish Evangelical Mission Covenant of America. He died on August 4, 1937, in Chicago. For further reading see *Son of the People: The Autobiography of C.V. Bowman*.

Frans Oscar Kling was born in Västernorrlands län, Sweden, on February 10, 1873. He immigrated to America in 1893 and graduated from North Park Seminary in 1902; he also attended Union Theological College. He was ordained by the Swedish Evangelical Mission Covenant of America in June 1903 in Minneapolis. On March 11, 1897, he was united in marriage to Ida Marion Nelson. They had four children: Norman Francis, Evangeline, Paul, and Wendell. In addition to serving at Salem from 1908 to 1911, he served churches in Norway, Michigan; Wyanette, Minnesota; Duluth, Minnesota; Los Angeles and Kingsburg, California; Edgewater Church, Chicago; Blue Island, Illinois; South Chicago; Topeka, Kansas; and Riverside Church, Kingsburg, California. He died in the Covenant Home in Tujunga, California, on October 23, 1952.

Carl Frederick Sandstrom was born on September 30, 1872, in Vedum,

Skarsbergs län, Västergötland, Sweden. The date of his immigration to America is unknown. He graduated from North Park Seminary in 1896 and was ordained by the Swedish Evangelical Mission Covenant of America. He was united in marriage to Augusta Peterson in 1897; the children born to that union were Einar, Inez, David, Dorothy, Paul, and Ruth. In addition to serving Salem from March 1912 to June 1920, he served churches in Manistee, Michigan; Seattle, Washington; Buffalo, Minnesota; Oakland and Kingsburg, California; and Lynn, Massachusetts. He died on December 2, 1932. For further reading see *Landmarks of the Spirit*, by David H. Sandstrom.

Carl Adolph Gavert was born in Söderbärkes parish, Dalarna, Sweden, on June 17, 1882. Following his conversion in 1898, he entered the Bible institute at Eskilstuna, and upon graduation served as an evangelist for the Swedish Mission Covenant. Immigrating to America in 1902, he lived in Bridgeport, Connecticut, and served as a lay preacher in the congregation there. He entered North Park College and Theological Seminary, graduating in 1907. In 1910 he was ordained by the Swedish Evangelical Mission Covenant of America in Salina, Kansas. On June 21, 1911, he was united in marriage to Amanda Christina Maenson in Fort Dodge, Iowa. They had three children: Dagmar Theodora, Paul Adolf, and Carma Audrine. In addition to serving Salem from July 1920 to October 1929, he served churches in Anaconda, Montana; Salina, Kansas; Sioux City, Iowa; Paxton, Illinois; and the Irving Park and Cragin churches in Chicago. While at Salem he taught at Minnehaha Academy and served on the school board. During his pastorate in Chicago he was director of a Swedish radio program and served as associate editor for *Missiönsvännen* (*The Mission Friend*). He died in Fort Dodge, Iowa, on September 20, 1958.

Clarence August Nelson was born on September 8, 1900, in St. Paul, Minnesota. His family were members of First Covenant Church, St. Paul, where he was baptized and confirmed by Rev. A.E. Palmquist and joined the church. He was a graduate of Minnehaha Academy, North Park College and Theological Seminary, and Macalaster College, St. Paul. He held an honorary doctor of divinity degree from Macalester, and was awarded a doctor of humane letters and a distinguished service citation from North Park College. In June 1960 he was awarded the Order of North Star by the king of Sweden. On October 27, 1926, he was united in marriage to Blanche Adeline Nordell in Minneapolis, to which union was born a son, Craig. In 1927 he was ordained by the Swedish Evangelical Mission Covenant of America at the Englewood Covenant Church of Chicago. In addition to serving Salem from November of 1929 to April of 1947, his pastoral and administrative duties were wide-ranging. His pastoral ministry included First Covenant, St. Paul, where he served as assistant pastor; Stillwater, Minnesota; and Evanston, Illinois. From 1943 to 1950 he was president of Minnehaha Academy, and from 1950 to 1959 he was president of North Park College and Theological Seminary. In 1959 he became as president of the Evangelical Covenant Church of America, serving until his retirement in 1967, when he was named president emeritus. In retirement he served interim pastorates at Bloomington and Excelsior, Minnesota. He died in Minneapolis on July 21, 1971, and his memorial service was held at Salem.

Clarence David Agard was born on October 4, 1911, in Chicago. His preparation for the ministry included the University of Wyoming, North Park Theological Seminary, and Valparaiso University. He was ordained by the Evangelical Covenant Church on April 19, 1942. On February 13, 1937, he was married to Evelyn M. Johnson in Chicago. They had four children: Bonnevieve Gale, Donald Wendell, Janice Evelyn, and Daniel Clarence. In addition to serving Salem from April of 1946 to February of 1959, he served the following churches: Chicago Heights, Illinois; San Diego, California; Lakeview Covenant, Chicago; Mt. Prospect, Illinois; Bethany Covenant, Lyndhurst, Ohio; Mt. Miguel Covenant, Spring Valley, California; and First Covenant, Sacramento, California. He served on the board of directors of North Park College and on the commission on ministerial training, and as chairman of the Northwest and Middle East conferences. He died at Spring Valley, California, on March 11, 1993.

Paul Earnest Stohlberg was born on February 10, 1927, at Stillwater, Minnesota. He graduated from North Park College, from Augsburg College in Minneapolis, and from North Park Theological Seminary in 1951. He was ordained by the Evangelical Mission Covenant Church of America on June 21, 1953, in Minneapolis. On August 27, 1949, he was married to Bernice Carlson at Stillwater, Minnesota. They had four children: Mark

Randall, Mary Ruth, Timothy Paul, and Elizabeth Ann. In addition to serving Salem from September 1959 to May 1978, he served at Winthrop, Minnesota (internship); Colony Church, Kingsburg, California; and Leyden Church, Denver, Colorado. In denominational and conference work, he served on the national board of Covenant youth work, on the Board of Ministerial Standing, and as vice-chairman of the Northwest Conference. He was chairman of the Minneapolis ministerial association and vice-president of the board of directors of the Greater Minneapolis Council of Churches. He died in Minneapolis on May 16, 1978.

Glen Vernon Wiberg was born on May 1, 1925, at Kansas City, Missouri. Following a lifelong sense of calling, he began his educational preparation for the ministry at Moody Bible Institute, Chicago; he then attended North Park College and William Jewell College, Liberty, Missouri. Following graduation from North Park Seminary in 1951, he pursued further studies at Yale Divinity School, New Haven, Connecticut, where in 1957 he received the master of divinity degree. On June 10, 1949, he was married to Jane Mabes, to which union were born three children: Katherine Ruth, Carl Eric, and Sarah Jane. He was ordained by the Evangelical Mission Covenant Church on June 21, 1953, in Minneapolis. He served the following churches: First Covenant, Oakland, California (internship); East Hampton, Connecticut; Princeton, Illinois; Youngstown, Ohio; North Park, Chicago; and Salem from February 1979 to his retirement in December 1991. Since retirement he has served interim pastorates at Trinity church, Salem, Oregon; Bethlehem, Minneapolis; and North Park, Chicago. He has served on the denominational Board of Publication, the Board of Ministerial Standing, and the Covenant Executive Board, where he was vice-president of the denomination for two terms. He has served on the hymnal commissions for *The Covenant Hymnal* (1973) and *The Covenant Hymnal: A Worshipbook* (1996), and on the committees for *The Covenant Book of Worship* (1981) and the hymnal supplement *The Song Goes On* (1990). He is the author of the confirmation text *Called to be His People* (1970). On January 23, 1994, he was honored with the title of pastor emeritus of Salem. He resides in New Brighton.

Present Pastor

Don Norbert Johnson was born on March 18, 1953, in Chicago. He graduated from North Park College in 1976 and from North Park Theological Seminary in 1980. On August 27, 1975, he was married to Martha Anne Ensign in Mechanicsville, Virginia. They have three children: Isaac Don, Luke Timothy, and Elizabeth Ruth. He was ordained by the Evangelical Covenant Church on June 25, 1981, at Columbus, Ohio. In addition to serving Salem from August 1992 to the present, he served at Northbrook, Illinois (youth pastor); Osage City, Kansas (internship); Lafayette, Indiana; and Muskegon, Michigan. He was chairman of the Covenant Board of World Mission, and served on the centennial fund drive steering committee and the Central Conference Education and Leadership Commission. He served as vice-chairman of the Central Conference executive board, as a member of the trustee board of the Great Lakes Conference, and as vice-chairman of that conference's ministerium.

Interim Pastors

Carl Oscar Nelson was born on May 28, 1879, in the parish of Virserum, Småland, Sweden. Immigrating to America in his youth, he attended Macalester College, St. Paul, and Wesleyan University, Helena, Montana. He graduated from North Park Seminary in 1907. Following his graduation, he served as interim pastor at Salem from 1907 to 1908. He was ordained by the Swedish Evangelical Mission Covenant of America in 1910 at Springfield, Massachusetts. On July 14, 1914, he was married to Lillian E. Carlson, to which union were born two children: Ruth and James Theodore. In addition to the interim at Salem, he served as pastor at Duluth, Minnesota; Springfield, Massachusetts; Red Wing, Minnesota; and Whitehall, Michigan. He also served interim pastorates at Fitchburg, Massachusetts, and Cheboygan, Michigan. He died at Cromwell, Connecticut, on January 5, 1969.

Joel Sigfrid Johnson was born on February 16, 1876, in Norra Vram, Malmöhus län, Skåne, Sweden. He immigrated to America in 1892 and completed his studies for the ministry at North Park College and Theological Seminary in 1902. He was ordained by the Swedish Evangelical Mission Covenant of America in 1904 at Lockport, Illinois. On January 20,

1914, he was married to Adine Wenberg. They had two children: Winston Sigfrid Allen and Jeanette Adelaid. His service in China spanned the years from 1904 to 1949. While on furlough he served as interim pastor at Salem from 1911 to 1912 between the pastorates of F.O. Kling and Carl Sandstrom. From 1927 to 1931, when missions in China were closed to Americans, he served as secretary of missions in the Covenant. During World War II he was held prisoner by the Japanese for eighteen months. From 1952 to 1955 he served as missions representative in the California and North Pacific conferences. Prior to his missionary service, he served as pastor in Lockport and Chicago Heights, Illinois. He died in Seattle, Washington, on February 5, 1973.

Norbert Edwin Johnson was born on April 6, 1925, at Gladstone, Michigan. Following three years in the Army during World War II, he went to the North Park College School of Music, graduating in 1948; he then transferred to the Conservatory of Music at Wheaton College and graduated in 1950. Sensing the call to ministry, he returned to North Park, graduating from the seminary in 1953. While on sabbatical in 1969-70, he earned the master of theology degree in church history from Union Seminary, Richmond, Virginia. On June 17, 1950, he was married to Elaine Larson in Iron Mountain, Michigan. They have three children: Don Norbert, Carolyn Christal, and Timothy Burton. He was ordained by the Evangelical Mission Covenant Church in June of 1952 at Worcester, Massachusetts, and has served the following churches: Carlshend, Michigan (summer pastor); Layfayette, Indiana; First Covenant, St. Paul; First Covenant, Omaha; and North Park, Chicago. From January to April of 1992 he served as interim pastor at Salem. He has served on the Board of Publication, the board of directors of North Park College and Seminary, and the Covenant Executive Board, where he was also liaison to the Board of Ministry.

Wallace Harvey Pratt was born on November 12, 1926, in Minneapolis, Minnesota. He graduated from Augsburg College in 1951, attended Luther Theological Seminary, and graduated from North Park Seminary in 1954. He also took post-graduate work at the San Diego Institute of Pastoral Counseling. He was ordained by the Evangelical Covenant Church in 1956 at Chicago. On March 19, 1948, he was married to Lorraine Bjorklund at Salem on 18 1/2 and Central avenues, and to this union were born five children: Leonard Wallace, Lowell Harvey, Joyce Lorraine, Sharon Linnea, and Warren Nathaniel. He served as student pastor at Calumet Park, Illinois, and upon graduation from seminary was called to Red Wing, Minnesota. He also served in Spring Valley, California, and Dassel, Minnesota. From 1963 to 1966 he served as chaplain at Minnehaha Academy. Following his retirement, he was called as interim pastor at Salem from May through September of 1992. He served as secretary of the Northwest Conference and on the national Board of Ministry, the Covenant Commission on World Relief, the Board of Benevolence, and the Covenant Retirement Communities of Minnesota management committee. He is presently serving at Salem as minister of outreach and visitation

Associate Pastors

Karl Edgar Johnson was born on August 15, 1932, in Chicago, Illinois. He graduated from Wheaton College in 1954 and continued his studies for the ministry in the Graduate School of Theology at Wheaton. He then transferred to North Park Theological Seminary, from which he graduated in 1959. On September 15, 1962, he married Constance Taylor in Minneapolis. They have two children: Karla Louise and Carleton Elmer. On June 25, 1961, he was ordained by the Evangelical Covenant Church of America at Chicago. In addition to serving as associate pastor at Salem from June of 1958 to September of 1962, he served pastorates in Portage, Indiana; New Britain, Connecticut; and Edgebrook, Chicago. Since 1983 he has been director of development and public relations at Covenant Children's Home and Family Services in Princeton, Illinois.

Lloyd Ashley Larsen was born on July 4, 1936, at Evanston, Illinois. He graduated from North Park College, Augustana College in Rock Island, Illinois, and North Park Theological Seminary. He was ordained by the Evangelical Covenant Church of America in June of 1964 in Minneapolis. On June 11, 1960, he was married to Janet C. Baker, to which union were born three children: Ann Jo, Sarah Lynn, and Andrea Lea. In addition to serving as associate pastor at Salem from September 1962 to September 1966, he served his internship at First Covenant, Denver, Colorado, and as youth director at First Covenant, Moline, Illinois. His ordination standing was transferred to the United Church of Christ on June 18, 1970.

Karl Wesley Olson was born on February 10, 1930, at Bird Island, Minnesota. His educational preparation for the ministry included North Park College and North Park Theological Seminary, from which he graduated in 1954. He pursued further education at Northern Illinois University in DeKalb, the University of Minnesota, and Luther Northwestern Theological Seminary in St. Paul. He was ordained by the Evangelical Mission Covenant Church of America on June 24, 1956. On June 29, 1951, he was married to Harriet Louise Settergren, to which union were born four children: Lynda Mae, DiAnn Louise, Kent Wesley, and Brenda Joy. In addition to serving as associate pastor and later as acting senior pastor between the years of 1967 and 1979, he served at First Covenant, Duluth, Minnesota (youth pastor); Barrett and Lowry, Minnesota; Elgin, Illinois; Roseville Church, St. Paul; and Mankato, Minnesota. His activities in conference and denominational work are wide-ranging, including serving on the national Board of Ministry and, since August 1, 1986, as superintendent of the Midwest Conference.

Frances Delores Decker was born on July 2, 1928, at Maple Lake, Minnesota. Her educational background includes St. Paul Bible College, St. Cloud State College, New York University, North Park College, and Bethel Theological Seminary in St. Paul. She was ordained by the Evangelical Covenant Church on June 21, 1986, in Chicago. In addition to serving at Salem as minister of Christian education and associate pastor from 1980 to 1992, she was director of Christian education at the Brookdale Covenant Church in Minneapolis, teacher at St. Paul Bible College, and assistant director of Christian education for the Covenant, in which role she was also director of field services and mobile ministries. She has also served nationally on the Board of Benevolence and the ministerium. She is presently serving as chaplain at Bethany Covenant Home, Minneapolis.

James Leonard Anderson was born on February 18, 1950, at St. Paul, Minnesota. He graduated from the University of Minnesota in 1972 and from North Park Theological Seminary in 1977. On December 29, 1972, he was married to Sally J. Anderson at St. Paul, to which union were born two children: Britt Elizabeth and Rachel Ingrid. He was ordained by the

Evangelical Covenant Church on June 8, 1978. In addition to serving Salem as associate pastor from May of 1983 to September of 1991, he did his internship at Foster City, Michigan, served as associate pastor and later as senior pastor of the Trinity Covenant Church, Salem, Oregon, and since September 1991 has served as pastor of the newly established Shoreview Covenant Church. In the Northwest Conference he has served on the Covenant Pines camp board, the Board of Ministerial Standing, and as vice-chairman of the Twin Cities Covenant ministerium

Visitation Pastors

Andor Elvin Smedberg was born on September 2, 1887, in Sundsvall, Sweden. Upon immigrating to America, he attended and graduated from North Park College and Theological Seminary and was ordained by the Swedish Evangelical Mission Covenant of America in Minneapolis in 1917. He was married to Naima A. Konradson, and to this union were born four children: Ebba Louise Kristine, Dagmar Cecelia, Roland Andor, and Elvin Emanuel. In addition to serving churches in Tiskilwa and Stillman Valley, Illinois; Menominee, Michigan; Salem, Duluth, Minnesota; and First, San Diego, California, he served in his earlier years as an evangelist in Sweden and later as director of the Kallman Home for Children in Brooklyn, New York. He served interim pastorates at Camden, Minneapolis; Elim, St. Paul; and Floral Park, New York. From October 1944 to May 1946 he served as visitation pastor at Salem, conducting Sunday morning services in Swedish in the lower auditorium. He died on October 13, 1959.

George Holmberg served as visitation pastor from 1958 to 1959, but his credentials were apparently non-Covenant and therefore no biographical data is presently available. Older members recall that he may have been a missionary under the Scandinavian Alliance Mission (now TEAM).

Elmer Bernard Dahlstrom was born on June 21, 1895, at St. Hilaire, Minnesota. He attended Minnehaha Academy, North Park College and Theological Seminary, and the University of California at Berkeley. He was ordained by the Swedish Evangelical Mission Covenant of America on June 26, 1932, in Grantsburg, Wisconsin. On June 10, 1933, he was married to Violet Christine Lundquist, and to this union were born four children: Robert, Donald, Carole Ann, and Kathryn Ann. He served churches in Harris, Minnesota; Lily Lake, Illinois; Berkeley, California; Grantsburg and Siren, Wisconsin; Worthington, Minnesota; Lanyon, Iowa; Greeley, Colorado; Harcourt and Dayton, Iowa; and an interim in Hastings, Nebraska. He served as superintendent in the Midwest Conference and on the Covenant Board of World Mission and Board of Ministerial Standing. His service as visitation pastor at Salem was from 1966 until his death on March 20, 1967.

Axel Milton Freedholm was born on February 7, 1899, in Chicago, Illinois. He attended the University of Chicago, North Park Theological Seminary, and the University of Minnesota. On June 19, 1928, he was married to Esther Elizabeth Anderson, who died on April 27, 1929. Subsequently, on May 28, 1932, he was united in marriage to Helen J. Port, to which union were born two children: Arlene Helen and Herbert Milton. On September 13, 1936, he was ordained by the Swedish Evangelical Mission Covenant of America. He served at Parkside, Chicago, at First Church in Denver, Colorado, and for over forty years at Bethlehem Covenant Church, Minneapolis. In his retirement he served as associate pastor at Bethesda in Rockford, Illinois, and from September 1973 to June 1, 1978, as visitation pastor at Salem. His denominational service was wide-ranging, including dean of Minnehaha Academy, Covenant archivist, the Covenant Executive Board, the boards of publications, missions, and pensions, the Music Commission, and numerous other commissions. He died on October 9, 1986, in Minneapolis.

Nathan John Sundberg was born on February 9, 1909, in Stromsburg, Nebraska. He attended Northwestern University in Evanston, Illinois, and North Park Theological Seminary, where he graduated in 1939. On June 10, 1939, he was united in marriage to Evangeline Youngquist, also of Stromsburg. To this union were born five children: Leland Paul, Lois Evangeline, Stanley Waldon, Miriam Christine, and Mark Jonathan. He was ordained by the Swedish Evangelical Mission Covenant of America in Aurora, Nebraska, in 1942, and served churches in Aurora and in Albert City, Iowa; Fridley, Minnesota; Buffalo, New York; and Bethesda, Rockford, Illinois, where he served as visitation pastor. He served in a similar pastoral role at Salem from 1980 to 1982. He died in Minneapolis on August 3, 1982.

Donald Bernhard Krause was born on August 12, 1925, in Milwaukee, Wisconsin. He attended Marquette University in Milwaukee, Northwestern College in Minneapolis, and Southern Illinois University in Carbondale, Illinois; and he graduated from North Park College and Theological Seminary in 1955. He was ordained by the Evangelical Covenant Church on June 24, 1956, at Chicago. On June 11, 1949, he was married to Betty Ann Nokleby, and to this union were born two sons: Thomas Evans and Todd Donald. He served churches at Randall and Alexandria, Minnesota; Maplewood, St. Paul; and Bensonvale, Omaha, Nebraska . He has also served as chaplain at the Anna State Hospital, Anna, Illinois; and at Swedish Hospital (later Metropolitan Medical Center), Fairview (Southdale), and North Memorial Hospital, all in Minneapolis. Earlier he served as administrative assistant at Minnehaha Academy. A longstanding member of Salem, he was called as visitation pastor in 1992. He and Betty currently reside in New Brighton.

Wallace Harvey Pratt, whose biographical data is given above, was called as visitation pastor in 1992 and continues to serve in that capacity.

Appendix B

Church Officiary

Church Officiary

Congregational Chairpersons

1888-1894	A.G. Erickson
1894-1895	Andrew Rosen
1895-1905	John Olson
1905-1924	Charles G. Larson
1925-1929	John Gustafson
1930-1933	Andrew Kylander
1933-1936	Frans Lundberg
1936-1942	Albert Holm
1942-1945	Edward T. Johnson
1945-1948	Austin Frisk
1948-1951	Walfred Jacobson
1951-1955	Ewald Beckstrom
1955-1958	Harlan Erickson

1959-1961	William Goolsbee
1961-1964	Harold Lundeen
1964-1967	Ward Holm
1967-1970	V. Laurie Peterson
1970-1973	Norman Engman
1973-1975	James Redeske
1975-1977	Russell Lorenson
1977-1980	Ronald Johnson
1980-1981	Glen Bjorklund
1981-1984	Mark Stohlberg
1984-1987	Alan DeVries
1987-1990	David Larson
1990-1993	Judy Edlund
1993-present	Robert Sundquist

Parish Workers and Church Secretaries

1911-1936	Alma Johnson
1937-1943	Erma Chinander
1943-1946	Dorothy Lundstrom Balch
1946-1948	Lorraine Bjorklund Pratt
1948-1968	Olga Gustafson
1962	June Abrahamson
1964	Darlene Knecht
1968-1981	Carolyn Fisher
1978-1981	Norma Grosch
1981-1985	Elsie Hoffman
1983-1987	Jean Kelly
1986-1994	Betty Belohlavek
1987-1994	Sally Anderson
1984-present	Karen Bjorklund

Sunday School Superintendents and School of Christian Living

1882-1887	Frans Larson
1887-1915	L.M. Lindquist

1979-1982	Terry Sheetz
1983-1984	Peter Hanslep
1984-present	Terry Sheetz

Organists

1888-1889	John E. Merricks
1889-1895	Augusta Frisk
1895-1897	Axel Wallin
1897	Olaf Holmer
1897-1902	Oscar Johanson
1902-1924	Joseph Burns
1925-1930	Reuben Lundstrom, Amy Nelson
1930-1935	Elton Bjorklund
1935-1944	Helga Holmer, Amy Nelson
1944-1947	Wayne Balch
1948-1950	Janet Carlson Gassler
1951-1957	Gordon Ahlquist
1957-1958	Barbara Peterson Smith, Elaine Lundstrom Ahlstedt
1958-1962	David Babcock
1962-1964	Shirley Mogck
1965-1971	Barbara Lord Collings
1971-1973	Jan Arthur
1974-1975	Mary Lindahl
1976-present	Cindy Wobig Reents

Musical Groups

Because of the importance of music in the life and worship of Salem throughout its history, many musical groups have given voice to the congregation's song. Some groups have been of short duration, while others have lasted much longer. Two of the earliest musical organizations were the male chorus and string band organized in 1894. While not having a continuous history, the male chorus made significant contributions to the musical life of Salem under the leadership of John Stone at the turn of the century, Reuben Lundstrom in the twenties, and J. Helmer Stattine in the thirties. On special occasions, such as church anniversaries, the male chorus has resurfaced.

In a similar way the string band was a strong musical group in earlier years, and in the twenties it flourished under Amanda (Mrs. C.A.) Gavert, Amy Nelson, and C.H. Kjellberg. For the ninetieth anniversary in 1978 the string band was revived by Norman Hoglund. Under the leadership of Lester Schwartz it continues to be a vigorous group, playing at the yearly Christmas smörgåsbord and giving concerts throughout the area.

A ladies' choir was organized in the twenties under the direction of Olga (Mrs. Eric) Bergman, but appears to have been short-lived. In more recent years the Salem Swedish Singers (including several male singers) under the direction of Marillyn Goolsbee, has performed yearly at the smörgåsbord in December and for other groups throughout the city.

A string orchestra begun in 1900 under the direction of John Nelson made an important contribution to the musical life of Salem. Likewise, a youth orchestra in more recent years was organized and led by Betty Krause and later directed by Sandra Collins. Youth and children's choirs have had a significant ministry in the congregation, with groups such as Peace in Light under the direction of Ron White and, more recently, the Strong Foundation under the leadership of Larry Babb. Children's music has been well served by LaVonne Ecker, Mary Lou Tidman, Joyce Colotti, Dawn Savat, and Marilyn Jenson. In the late 1980s a bell choir was formed and led by Loreda Johnson, who was followed by a succession of directors including Larry Oberg, Mary Lou Tidman, Helen Olson, Lynn Erickson, and Heidi Sawyer.

Providing a continuum through the years has been the church choir, more recently referred to as the Sanctuary Choir. The names listed above as directors, beginning with Axel Wallin in 1895 and continuing with the skilled musicianship of Joseph Burns for twenty-two years (1902-1924), profoundly shaped the finest church music available in worship and in concerts presenting the classics both old and new.

The History Book Committee offers its apology for any names or groups omitted from this brief summary.

Appendix C

Centennial Events of 1988

An overview of Salem's centennial year from planning to fulfillment has been recorded in minutes, orders of service, programs, letters of greeting, and other artifacts kept by the co-chairpersons of the centennial committee, Jerry and Elaine Green. This record is preserved and available in the church archives. Other members of the committee appointed by the church council were Erma Chinander, Phyllis Erickson, Curtiss D. Johnson, Bernice Stohlberg, Evelyn Strand, Al and Marilyn Tengvall, and Pastor Glen V. Wiberg.

The first meeting of the committee was held at the home of the Greens in September 1986, when ideas and plans for the observances were discussed. These ideas included musical events, commemorative items, a budget, and a centennial theme. The theme chosen was "Lift High the Cross," which also became the theme song for the year. Prior to that initial meeting, contact had been made with Curtis L. Carlson, chairman of New Sweden 88—an event in the planning stage that would commemorate the contributions of Swedish background churches to the cultural and religious life of Minnesota and the Twin Cities.

In early 1987 the committee stepped up its pace of regular meetings held in homes and at church, giving particular attention to musical events appropriate for the year of celebration. Contacts were made with the music commission to coordinate the presentation of choral music with distinguished soloists, organists, and other instrumentalists.

A service of worship inaugurating the centennial year on January 3,

1988, included music by the Salem Swedish Singers and the Sanctuary Choir, with Pastor Wiberg preaching on the theme "The Church with the Pail and Dipper says 'Come.'" On the following Sunday Erma Chinander paid tribute to missionary Martha Anderson, marking the fortieth anniversary of her martyrdom in China in January of 1948.

During the year several vignettes dramatically portraying Salem's history were presented as part of Sunday morning worship services:

- January 31, "Earliest Beginnings: This Side of the River"
- August 29, "Salem's Ministry to Service Personnel"
- September 18, "A Change of Language for Salem's Ministry"
- December 18, "The Move to the New Church"

On September 13, at the first fall meeting of Covenant Women, a vignette entitled "Bridging the Decades" portrayed in costume and script the role of women in Salem. Because of their historic value, these vignettes have been preserved in the church archives.

Musical events during the year included a choral service of tenebrae on Good Friday, with the Sanctuary Choir singing "The Seven Last Words" by DuBois; an organ recital by Cindy Reents on May 15 commemorating the tenth anniversary of Pastor Paul E. Stohlberg's death; a concert preceding the morning service on July 26 by opera singer Stephen Swanson, from Germany, son of Phoebe and Richard Swanson; and an organ recital on August 11 by Winston Johnson of Seattle, Washington, son of missionary Joel Johnson.

Another outstanding musical event was the visit by the Immanuel Church choir from Stockholm, Sweden, on the weekend of October 8, with a concert Saturday evening and selections offered in the Sunday services. The choir also came to participate in the New Sweden '88 celebration along with Walter Persson, president of the Swedish Mission Covenant. The choir was directed by Ingemar Braennstroem, with soloists Anders Andersson and Christina Östman. The pastor of Immanuel Church, Åke Hedström, also accompanied the tour and was guest preacher in Salem's pulpit. On Reformation Sunday, October 30, the Minnesota Brassworks played in the services and accompanied congregational singing.

Other memorable people closely associated with Salem were invited to participate in the year's observances, including Mary Mae Erickson, daughter of Freda Klinka, first matron of Bethany Home, who shared her reflections and memories on April 10, and Craig W. Nelson, president of Minnehaha Academy and a son of the congregation, who returned to preach at the services on Sunday, September 18.

A special weekend of October 15 and 16 was dedicated to a missions fair and a missions Sunday, with guest preacher Raymond Dahlberg, former youth pastor at Salem and currently executive secretary of Covenant world mission. Following the worship service on October 16, three commemorative stained glass panels were dedicated in Fellowship Hall, including a panel in memory of missionary Martha Anderson.

A confirmation reunion was held on September 17, providing opportunity for welcoming back to Salem many who experienced the confirming of baptismal promises and faith in Christ during their early youth. Chairman of the event Terry Bjorklund reported that 310 people responded from the classes of 1907 through 1976. Speakers were Rev. Erick Gustafson (1920), Anna Koester (1928), and James Bengtson (1967). On November 19 a centennial banquet took place in the social hall, with Pastor Clarence Agard of San Diego, California, sharing reflections of his ministry at Salem. On the following Sunday, November 20, Paul E. Larsen, president of the Evangelical Covenant Church, was guest preacher.

The final official event of the year was a birthday party on December 18 celebrating the date of founding, December 17, 1888. K. Wesley Olson, former associate pastor and subsequently superintendent of the Midwest Conference, was pulpit guest. The party was preceded December 11 by a choral presentation of Mendelssohn's Symphony No. 2, *The Hymn of Praise*, with soloists and instrumentalists directed by Terry Sheetz. It was an uplifting choral work, spirited in nature and appropriate as a musical tribute to the completion of Salem's one hundred years of ministry and the beginning of its next century of service to God and his kingdom.

When the centennial committee met on February 20, 1989, to review the activities of the year, the decision was made to form a history book committee, with Curtiss D. Johnson volunteering to serve as chairman. The story *This Side of the River* flows out of a memorable year of remembrance and hope.

Appendix D
In Memorium

Blessed are the dead who die in the Lord. Blessed indeed, says the Spirit, that they may rest from their labors, for their deeds follow them."—*Revelation 14:13*

Gifts have been received by sponsors for the history book of the Salem centennial in memory of the following persons:

Alton H. Abrahamson
Hjalmer and Alma Abrahamson
Kurt Abrahamson
Pastor Clarence Agard
Melvin Ahlberg
Pastor Adolph and Annette Anderson
Eva Anderson
Gustaf A. and Barbara Anderson
Marvin E. Anderson
Paul W. Anderson
Karl and Ruth Andersson
Bergith Atkinson
Leslie Bakke
Ewald and Angela Beckstrom
Warren Beckstrom
Adolph and Gustava Bergdahl
Ruth Bergquist
Arthur and Esther Bjorklund
Melvin Bjorklund
Norman and Mae Bjorklund
Godfried A. and Sofia Mathilda Bolin
Evelyn Borgstrom
Pastor Carl Victor Bowman
Joseph and Anna Burns
Sidney Burns
Lorraine Buzzell
Leroy and Marie Cannon
Nels Cannon
Aaron and Minnie Carlson
Carl A. and Sophia C. Carlson
Victor and Josephine Carlson
Wallace Carlson

Edward and Anna Chalgren
Sarah Cunningham
Jeanette Dahl
Larney and Millrose Dahl
Albert L. Dillon
Esther Eclov
Ann Engman
Arthur G. and Mattie Erickson
Arthur W. Erickson
Charles F. and Mathilda Erickson
Dale Erickson
Harlan I. Erickson
Esther Kjellberg Franzen
John Gable
Pastor Carl A. and Amanda Gavert
Bernice Green
Richard and Hazel Green
Swan A. and Anna Green
Henry and Ethel Gustafson
Walter and Olga Gustafson
Marion R. Hagman
Norman Hoglund
Albert and Elizabeth Holm
Axel Holm
Donald Holm
Nels Holm
Valborg Holm
Carl Holmer
Edla Holmer
Helga Holmer
Randall Holmer
Rudolph and Mildred Jenson
Vera Jernall
Carl P. Johnson
David and Augusta Johnson
Edward T. and Florence M. Johnson
Elmer and Violet Johnson
Gordon R. Johnson
Hilding and Jenny Johnson
Pastor Joel S. and Adine Johnson
John M. and Lydia W. Johnson
Lennert W. Johnson
Lloyd and Dora Johnson
Pastor Karl A. and Ellen Jonson
Freda Klinka
Edward and Olga Knight
Donald Knight
Andrew and Julia Kylander
David E. Lindholm
Lillian Cannon Lundberg
Agda Lundgren
Erick and Amanda Lundquist
Reuben and Ruth Lundstrom
Louisa Lunquist
Eleanor Joyce Maas
Richard and Ethel Monson
Dwight Nash
Amy Nelson
Dr. Clarence A. Nelson
John Fred and Betsy Nelson
Oscar and Nellie Nelson
Edith Newquist
Louis and Augusta Newquist
Raymond and Gladys Newquist
Robert (Bob) Newquist
Erick and Ella Nordeen
Stanley Nordeen
Gladys Nordeen Peterson

John and Carrie Nordstrom
George O. Nygaard
George Oberg
Charles and Kristina Olson
Eng and Anna E. Olson
Mabel Olson
Albert and Lydia Peterson
Charles and Betty C. Peterson
David G. Peterson
Hazel Peterson
Stanley and Alice Peterson
Victor and Amy Peterson
Lawrence C. Pratt
Carl F. and Hulda Resberg
Ella Roggeman
Carl L. and Mathilda Rosell
Donald (Bud) and Gladys Rosell
Pastor Carl Frederick Sandstrom
Andrew and Augusta Skoog
Adolph and Lillian Soderlund
Agnes Cannon Spellman
Agnes E. Strand
Glen B. Strand
Eldon Strandine
Pastor Paul E. Stohlberg
Arthur and Edith Swanson
Francis Tengvall
William and Beulah Terry
John and Lillian Twedt
George Wainio
Charles and Alma Wall
Lawrence Wall
Axel and Helen Wallentine
Gordon A. Wallentine
James and Ruth Resberg Ward
Carl Eric Wiberg
Theodore and Anna Youngberg

Sponsors

David and June Abrahamson, Inez Abrahamson, Nancy Abrahamson and family, Perry and Jeannette Adamson, Bonnie Agard, Lenore Ahlberg, Jerome and Elaine Ahlstedt, Beatrice Anderson-Welch, Dorothy Twedt Anderson, George and Margaret Anderson, Paul and Marion Anderson, Ronald and Judith Anderson, W. Dorothy Anderson, Karl Andersson, Neoma L. Bakke, Wayne and Dorothy Balch, Glen and Betty Bjorklund, Orville and Alpha Bjorklund, Donald Buzzell, Esther Buzzell, Paul Carlson, Roger and Mildred Carlson, Dorothy Soderlund Dyson, Mary Mae Klinka Erickson, Myrna Erickson, Phyllis Erickson, Elizabeth Fratzke, Douglas and Kathleen Frisk, William and Marillyn Goolsbee, Alvin and Bernice Green, Curtis H. and Marge Green, Terri Gulliford, Robert and Lorraine Hammerstrom, Carrie Hoglund, Beryl Holm, Paul and Phyllis Holmer, Frances Howard, Peter and Gladys Howell, Bonnie L. Johnson, Curtiss D. and Lorraine Johnson, Douglas and Judith Johnson, Evelyn M. Johnson,

G. Robert Johnson, Harold and Geneva Johnson, Richard and Elaine Johnson, Ronald and Ann Johnson, Vern and Betty Johnson, Winston and Irma Johnson, Henry and Carol Kjellberg, William and Ruth Larson, Fred and Bonnie Leonard, Loren and Rita Lindholm, Harold and Edith Lundeen, Arthur and Muriel Lundell, Verna Lundgren, Frank and Nanette Lunquist, Arno and Ione Chalgren Martin, John Marwin, Jeanne M. Mason, Vernice Monson, Blanche Nelson, Craig and Betty Nelson, Esther Nygaard, Ruby Oberg, Keith and Alpha Olson, Kellogg and Maxine Olson, Kermit and Donna Olson, Nils William and Dagmar Olsson, Jack L. and Ruth Patton, Allan and Barbara Peterson, Frances Peterson, Russell and Joyce Peterson, V. Laurie and Ardis Peterson, Wallace and Lorraine Pratt, Lester and Jeanette Schwartz, J Russell and Karen Shannon, Richard and Marlys Sjoblom, Helen Smith, Bernice Stohlberg, Evelyn Strand, Alpha Strandine, Alvin and Marilyn Tengvall, Gary and Debbie Thalin, Curtis and Sharon Wall, Doris Wallentine, Glen and Jane Wiberg, Dorothy Youngberg

Gifts have also been received from Terri Gulliford and Julie Ann Jakubowski in honor of Paul and Aaron E. Carlson, grandsons of Aaaron and Minnie Carlson and sons of C. Albert Carlson; and from the Men's Brotherhood yearly smörgåsbord and the Salem String Band.